With New and Open Eyes

Wayne Brouwer

Seven Worlds Corporation
P. O. Box 11565
Knoxville, TN 37939

WITH NEW AND OPEN EYES

ISBN: 0-936497-10-6   Paperback $11.95

Seven Worlds Corporation
P. O. Box 11565
Knoxville, TN 37939

Library of Congress Cataloging-in-Publication Data

Brouwer, Wayne

WITH NEW AND OPEN EYES, Wayne Brouwer

1st edition
p. 160
ISBN 0-936497-10-6
Publication Number:

Dedication

In memory of Ken Karsten
(1959 - 1993)
for whom "Honor Roll"
became a prophetic tribute.

Forward

The late British evangelist David Watson used to delight in telling a story about a widely respected businessman who was much in demand as a conference speaker. The success of this fellow was due, in no small part, to his secretary of many years who not only kept his schedule and relieved him of many taxing duties, but who also, over the years, had begun to understand both his work and his speaking style. To such an extent had they become a team that he was often able to toss off to her a few suggestions about a future speech, and she would prepare an outline and manuscript for him.

Of course, here's where the teamwork broke down. He received the acclaim while she struggled alone with hardly a word of thanks. Until one day, as he was flitting by between meetings, he stopped at her desk long enough to grab the draft she had prepared for his next speech, just moments away. He stuffed the sheaf of papers into his briefcase and rushed off to his appointment. A packed house greeted him as he was lavishly introduced. He took the prepared speech and began to address his expectant audience. It was a brilliant beginning. The theme and ideas were laid out succinctly, with humor and grace. Page one ended spritely, "And now, let me unfold this perspective for you further under seven headings."

He turned to page two. The page was blank except for one handwritten line from the pen of his slighted secretary, "You're on your own now!"

When I first made a quivering speech at a youth retreat two decades ago, I already felt both the pain and embarrassment of a moment like that. When one musters up the incredible audacity to speak to a crowd, there is an inescapably focused loneliness: "You're on your own now!" I marvel again, every Sunday, that people actually hand a multitude of moments over to me and allow me to stand alone at the conscious center of their thoughts and activities. Within me it produces great pain and anxiety, for I am not by nature a person for spotlights of any kind.

At the same time there wells up in me great embarrassment. For, even though I spend much time and effort in the preparation of the messages I bring, I know full well that I am indebted to many others for both inspiration and content. I do not have a secretary who forms and shapes my sermons. But let me discuss, briefly, under seven headings, some of those who are responsible for the materials in this book.

First, there is God. I am a reluctant preacher, carried backwards by divine urgings into a ministry I wouldn't have chosen for myself. However, I am not reluctant about my faith. It is often weak, often wary, often wandering, often weary; but it is also the source of my identity. I remember sitting in church as a young person and thinking how grand and wonderful it is to be brushed softly with the love of God, and yet how boring preaching seemed. The incongruence overwhelmed me, at times, and I had difficulty putting next to each other great grace and what I saw to be the stilted expressions of ecclesiastical self-preservation. Now that I am older, I understand better how God and the church fit together in this strange marriage partnership. But still I have made a conscious pledge to communicate God's grace with some degree of passion whenever the occasion arises. I hope that comes through in the messages included in this volume.

Second, there are "the truly great," as Stephen Spender put it in his marvelous poem. There are the preachers of the past and present who have whispered life into my spirit and who have shouted wonder around me. My bookshelves are lined with their blessings. I could name names, but too many would be left out, and others would be misunderstood, for they are of many different faiths and perspectives. Let me say that little, if anything, contained in this volume is "original." The structures and musings are mine, but the substance has been mulled over and disseminated by geniuses on whose shoulders I stand as a dwarf. Third, I pay tribute to my congregation here in London, for whom these messages were prepared. My call to ministry here came as a sudden surprise to most of the members, as it did to me. But ours has been a remarkable relationship. Some members left our church, saying that sermons such as these were not what they needed or expected; others have joined us in spite of the preaching they hear on Sundays; and many have been gracious enough to say that messages such as these have been helpful for the spiritual journeying of their lives. What is written on these pages was designed entirely with this congregation in mind. Publishing these messages now in book form is an afterthought. I am indebted to London First Christian Reformed Church for affirming whatever gifts I have in this ministry, and for structuring and developing the dimensions of the ministry team in a way that allows me often to concentrate my attentions on this work of wordsmithing the Word.

Fourth, I would be remiss if I did not mention by name my pastoral partner Peter Hogeterp. It was Peter who urged me, over the years, to focus my energies toward the worship and educational aspects of our shared ministry. I am truly blessed to have a colleague and pastor like him as friend and confidant.

Fifth, but certainly more prominent than numerical ordering would indicate, I must say thanks to my wife and daughters. Brenda knows me better than any other person, and encourages me to be more than I might otherwise imagine. And Kristyn, Kimberly, and Kaitlyn are constant reminders of the joy of life. The greatest thrill I can receive after a service of worship to the glory of God is a word of recognition from them that they knew, through the message, that I love God, and that He loves them.

Sixth, I must say a word of appreciation to the people at Seven Worlds Publishing, whose faces I don't know, and whose names are only casual signatures appended to many warm letters. I would not be publishing these messages if it were not for their insistence, along the way, that others might benefit from a collection such as this.

Finally, let me come full circle, and reiterate my indebtedness to God. My own spiritual journey has not been easy. I have known of God from my earliest thoughts, and I have feared and fretted about my relationship with Him over the years. But I have also come to enjoy the mystery of our encounters, far broader than acts of religious devotion alone. There is a wideness in His mercies that weaves the dangling strands of life into a fabric of grace and strength and beauty.

Let me add a postscript about the pages that lie ahead for you. Please remember that these documents were originally formed as manuscripts for public preaching. They are crafted in that style, and contain more "and's" and run-on sentences and incomplete phrases than would be the case if I were writing the same thoughts in literary fashion. It is tempting to edit these messages further (they have already been transformed from a carefully laid out "linear" form into these blocks of paragraphs) to make them look good and read well. But they were written to be read, and I secretly hope that maybe some of you will read at least portions of them out loud.

A final word. The title chosen for this book comes from a line in Thomas Traherne's lovely poem of faith called "The Approach:"

"But now with new and open eyes

I see beneath as if above the skies:
And as I backward look again
See all his thoughts and mine most clear and
plain;
He did approach, he me did woo;
I wonder that my God this thing would do."

I hope these pages convey to you my sense of wonder
about the things our God is doing.

Wayne Brouwer
Pentecost 1993

CONTENTS

On Catching the Wrong Bus!
Matthew 7:13-14

The newspapers in New York City once reported a strange story. A man bought a Greyhound ticket for Detroit, and he got on the bus. He sat down to read, and then he fell asleep for awhile. When he woke again, he talked with the other passengers, and he stretched his legs at the rest stop. Finally they pulled into the terminal, and he got off. He collected his bag, and then he asked someone how he could get to Woodward Avenue. But nobody knew! And he thought to himself: That's funny! So he tried again: How do I get to Woodward Avenue?! But nobody could help him! Nobody knew where Woodward Avenue was! Come on! he said. Woodward Avenue is Main Street here! I know Detroit! And then they exploded with laughter around him! This isn't Detroit! they said. This is Kansas City! He'd gotten on the wrong bus!

Did you ever do that? Catch the wrong bus? Or take the wrong turn? Sometimes it's no big deal. You just drive for a few minutes, and then you realize your mistake and you turn around and go back the other way. But sometimes it's a lot more serious than that. I spent the summer of 1977 in Alaska. I was serving as an intern at our Christian Reformed congregation in Anchorage. One family in the church had a rustic cabin out by a mountain lake. And they invited me to take all of the young people out there on a Saturday. There weren't that many young people, so we could all cram into a station wagon together like sardines. And then we set off. I didn't know where the place was, but little Gwen did. She was my navigator. Now, Alaska is a big place, quite a bit larger than the whole of Ontario. But it has only six highways. And just outside of Anchorage we had to take a turn, one way or the other. Gwen said left, so that's the way we went. An hour later I said to Gwen, for the tenth time, Are you sure this is the right way?! Do you recognize anything around here? And when we finally stopped for help, we were about as far away from where we wanted to be as we could be! We beat it back, all the way to that fork in the road near Anchorage. And when we finally got to the cabin, four hours late, they were beside themselves with anxiety. They didn't have a telephone, and they didn't know what had happened to us.

Catching the wrong bus. Taking the wrong turn. Those are just parables of life that illustrate the point of Jesus' words to us this morning: Enter through the narrow gate, he says. For wide is the gate and broad is the road that leads to destruction, and many enter through it. But small is the gate and narrow the road that leads to life, and only a few find it.

Now, what's he saying to us?

Well, for one thing, he's telling us that good intentions aren't enough in life. Remember Jesus' story of the Prodigal Son? He didn't start out looking for a job feeding pigs! That wasn't his intention at all! He collected his inheritance wealth, and he set out to find happiness, and freedom and friends and adventure! And those are noble wishes indeed! But then he got on the wrong bus. And when they showed him where he'd arrived, he knew the folly of his travels.

Sometimes I think of that as I'm officiating at a marriage ceremony. What a happy time! Everyone smiles! Everyone dresses to a T! Everything is so beautiful, so radiant, so full of hope and promise! And I stand up here with the bride and groom, and I see in their eyes the best of intentions: Theirs will be the perfect marriage! Theirs will be the strongest home! Theirs will be

2

the deepest vows, the truest commitments, the richest promises, the surest future! And yet there's within me this nagging uncertainty: They're headed for heaven ... Why, then, do some of them end up in hell? And I pray to God: Lord, let them get on the right bus!

Hector Berlioz, the famous composer...He was living in Paris in 1830, and he loved a young woman named Camille. They were engaged to be married. But then Hector was awarded the Prix de Roma, the Prize of Rome. He could study and compose and perform his music in Italy for a year or two, and all his financial needs would be covered! So off he went. He kissed Camille goodbye. His intentions never changed! Soon they'd be married, he said as he left. But life in Rome swallowed him up. And for Camille, life in Paris went on. Other suitors came. And when Berlioz next heard from her, she was on her way to marriage with another. So he caught the next coach to Paris. Only, he got on the wrong one, and ended up in Genoa. And then he tried again. Once more he booked passage to France. And he must have been in a daze, because he took the wrong coach again, and he ended up in Nice. And by this time Camille was married. And Berlioz quit his journey. That's what happens sometimes when you catch the wrong bus.

The world is full of good intentions! Nobody wants war! Everybody looks for prosperity! There's a hope and a wish and a desire for love in every human breast! But read the *Free Press*! Watch the National! Listen to the World at Six! The best of intentions isn't enough to heal the racial scars in Los Angeles right now! The highest ambitions can't lift the slums of Calcutta out of hell! The purest desires won't, by themselves, chart a course of peace and prosperity and democracy in the countries of the old Soviet Union! Having an ideal, catching the vision, knowing the city to which you want to go, doesn't get you there! You know the old saying: "The road to hell is paved with good intentions!" And that's what Jesus speaks of here.

Do you think that those who sit in A.A. meetings dreamed in their younger years that they would find themselves there? You know they didn't! And when they come to that point, when they find themselves in a city they didn't intend to visit, when they know that they took the wrong bus somewhere, what do they do? Do they wish for another city and imagine it into being? The city of Sobriety? The metropolis of Second Chances? Have you ever gone to an A.A. meeting? Then you know that the right bus comes for them only through hard work and only through mutual support and only through watching out for every step. They call each other, late at night. And they say to each other, Get on the right bus! Stay on the wagon! Don't let your thirst take your feet where your heart knows it shouldn't go!

You see, actions have consequences! When the Watergate scandal broke years ago, and President Nixon was forced to resign his office, Senator Sam Irvin of North Carolina said: "Do you know why this happened?" He said: "It happened because they forgot that actions have consequences."

Rudyard Kipling once wrote a poem about that. He called it "The Gods of the Copybook Headings." It was all about those little lessons we learned in elementary school, the ones that seemed so simple, but how important they were: that water will make us wet, and fire will burn us; that two and two are four, and pigs don't have wings; that all that glitters is not necessarily gold, and that the wages of sin are death. Says Kipling, "If we forget these fundamental rules of life, the Gods of the Copybook Headings with terror and slaughter shall return." And so it is. Actions have consequences. Good intentions aren't enough. Do you want to go to Detroit? Then get on the right bus! Do you want to make your dreams come true? Then enter the journey of life by the right gate!

That's the first thing this morning. And here's the second: **Every choice is a new gate!** Think of it! Hundreds, maybe thousands of people scattered there on the hillside around Jesus! And each is at a different stage of life. Some are grandmothers, with market bags in hand, watching the youngsters play in the meadow. Some are soldiers of fortune, marching in Palestine with the Roman legions because they wanted the taste of adventure, and they wanted to see the world. Some are poor folk, out scrounging the fields for tonight's meager eats. Some are educated teachers, and some are reluctant students. They're all here! And they all hear the words of Jesus; Find the right gate! Take the right bus! Make the right choices in life! And they can all act on Jesus' words, because every choice in life is a new gate.

C. S. Lewis described our lives so well in *Mere Christianity*. He has a chapter there called "Christian Behaviour." He talks about people who think that Christianity is sort of a one-time bargain with God: You do this for me, and I'll do that for you! And so we kind of bargain our way into heaven at the end, or maybe somewhere along the way. But no! says Lewis. That's not how Jesus looks at us! That's not the Bible's view of who we are! We aren't people who have managed to bargain our way into heaven! Do you know who we are? We're people who make choices. And we all start out here together, at one point, when we're tiny babies, on a place called earth. And then we start to choose: we go this way instead of that; we gather these friends instead of those; we pick this career rather than the other...And little by little, along the way, says Lewis, we begin to turn ourselves toward God, or toward something else, something far less, something ultimately demonic! And each choice in life is a new gate. Which way will you go?! No... Put it this way: Who are you becoming?!

Sometimes people ask me about knowing God's will. How do I know what God wants me to do in this situation? Does he want me to do this or to do that? Does he want me to go into medicine or accounting? How do I know? Let me tell you of a fellow I heard about. He loved two young women: Susan and Sharon. And he wanted to get married. But who should he marry? He wanted to do the right thing. So he played that little trick of Gideon, in the book of Judges. Gideon thought God wanted him to do something. But he wasn't sure. So he prayed real hard one night: God, if You want me to do this, then I'm going to make it easy for You to tell me. I'm going to put a big wooly fleece out tonight, and if You really want me to do this, then let the dew cover the ground, but let the fleece be completely dry! And that's what happened! And still Gideon wasn't sure. Even though he set the terms of the agreement! So that night he prayed again: Let's try it one more time, God! I'm not sure I heard You clearly last night. How about if we do something else tonight? Why don't you make the ground dry, and the fleece soaking wet with dew? So that's what God did. And now this young fellow, who liked both Sharon and Susan, wanted to pull a Gideon on God. So he took out a quarter. And he looked up toward heaven. And he said to God: Tell me who I should marry! Heads it's Susan, tails it's Sharon! And he tossed the coin into the air. And he caught it on his arm. And he looked under his palm. And he looked back to heaven, and he said: "How about two out of three?!"

Well, there you have it, don't you?! He's not really looking for God's will! He's looking for God to confirm <u>his</u> will! But the biggest problem with that is that God's will is rarely so small that it's merely this choice over that choice. God's will is a way of life, a series of choices, a decision that you keep on making! The two gates are always there in front of us! And it's not just a matter of picking up apples in the produce department, instead of oranges. It's always a question of values, of motives, of desires... Of seeing the goal of our lives in our minds, and then getting on the right bus, over and over and over again!

Says Lewis: "...every time you make a choice you are turning the central part of you, the part of you that chooses, into something a little different than it was before." He says, "When you look at your life as a whole, with all those innumerable choices you make from day to day all your life long you are slowly turning (yourself) either into a heavenly creature or into a hellish creature." It's not just Sharon or Susan! It's your life, your very soul! If you want love, then you can't have control! It's one or the other! It's this gate or that! Get on this bus, or wait for the next one! If you're looking for peace, then don't try coercion! You'll never find it! You'll be on the wrong bus! Do you want to find friends and conversation? Then you can't choose gossip! Those buses run on different schedules! Are you looking for God?! Then get on the right bus, again, and again, and again... At every stop along the road of your life!

Horace Bushnell was lecturing at Yale University long ago...And he had a crisis of faith. Was there really a God?! Could he talk about a faith he didn't feel?! How could he know the right way to go in his life?! And he stopped one day, and he looked toward the destination that he hoped to find, and he thought to himself: "This I know: that truth is better than a lie; that love is better than hate; that courage is better than cowardice. And so I will live for those things! Those are the choices I will make in my life!" That's the bus I will get on! And shortly before his death in 1876, he said to a friend (in Hartford, Connecticut): "I know Jesus Christ better than I know any man at Hartford." It didn't come for him by waltzing softly through life, by drifting along with the currents, by letting the winds blow him this way and that...It came for him each time he stood at the gates again, each time he had to make a choice in life, each time he got on a bus, and he looked to find the place where it was headed. And the choices of his life brought him round to God.

And that brings us round to the third thing this morning. Good intentions aren't enough in life. Every choice is a new gate. And here's the third thing: **Earlier decisions influence later decisions.**

Remember the poem by Robert Frost? He talks about finding himself in a forest of trees on a glorious Autumn afternoon. He's walking down a path. And then there's a fork in the way. Which direction should he go? And he makes his choice. And he picks his way. And he says to himself: "I shall be telling this with a sigh Somewhere ages and ages hence: Two roads diverged in a wood, and I--I took the one less traveled by, And that has made all the difference." And you know he's right! Years ago, you chose to settle in London, and see what's become of you for it?! You chose your course of education... Think of what you could have been if you'd have gone into engineering instead of medicine! But think also of who you've become because of the decision you made way back there! You chose your friends, and they've made you into something too! You chose your spouse, you chose your house, you chose this church...

And see what you've become because of it all! Because you chose medicine, you came to these fine hospitals here in London! Because you chose your friends, you've become more friendly, more loving, more trusting! Think of what you'd be like today, if you stayed in that crowd you used to run with! And because you chose this church, you've grown in Christ! You've learned, from this pulpit, of the grace of God, of the strength of holiness, of the joy of service and fellowship and commitment! Your earlier decisions have influenced you along the way.

George Mueller was one of the finest persons who ever walked this earth. In the last century, he set up orphanages around the world to care for the little ones who had no one to look after them. He provided for the poor. He preached the love of Christ, and he lived it every day. Someone once called him a success. He said no...He was only a servant, a servant of his master, the one who had loved him to life. Well, said the reporter, how did you manage to do all you've done during the course of your life. And George Mueller said: "I don't really know." He said: "As I look back on my life, I see that I was constantly brought to a crossroads which demanded a choice of which way I should go." And he said that once he had started to follow in the steps of Christ, all the rest of the decisions that came later seemed easier. He caught the right bus. And after he did it the first time, it was easier to find it the second time, and the third and the fourth and fifth and sixth. The earlier decisions made his later decisions easier.

Not so long ago, Robert Maynard, the author, had an article in the *New York Daily News*. He told of the time when he was young, and he was walking along to school one morning. And he came to a fresh patch of concrete in the sidewalk. Somebody had just finished trowelling it down nicely. It was just there waiting for him! So he bent down to write his name in the cement. And suddenly he saw this hulking shadow come over him! He looked up. And he saw the biggest mason he'd ever seen in his life! And the guy was holding a garbage can lid in his hand, ready to smash the first little kid who dared to mess up his new sidewalk! And Maynard says he tried to run, but the guy caught him around the waist. And he shouted: What do you think you're doing?! Why are you trying to spoil my work?! And Maynard says he remembers babbling something in his terror, something about only wanting to write his name there, for everyone to see. And the man's eyes softened. And he set young Maynard on the ground. And he said: Look at me, son! What do you want to be when you grow up?! And Maynard squeaked it out. He said: "A writer, I think!" And the man sat with him there for a moment. And then he pointed to the school across the street. And he said: "If you want to write your name where it really matters, then go to that school, and learn what it takes, and become a real writer. And then, someday, write your name on the cover of a book, and let the whole world see it!" And that, says Robert Maynard, is the day he became a writer. That was the day he made his decision. And every decision he's made since then has been easier. Because someone helped him to know who he really was. Because someone showed him how to make an early choice. Because someone took his hand at a critical moment in his life, and led him to the right bus.

And there's the focus of our service this morning. Why do we need to be concerned about the younger members of our congregation, and the education they receive? It's because the younger we are when we find the right bus in life, the easier it is to work our way through other crowded bus stations later on in our lives.

Earlier decisions influence later decisions. And no young child makes a right or wrong decision by himself or herself. He or she is led to that decision. By the hand. By the hand of some bigger person who says: this is what your life is all about. And if you want to find out what that means, then this is the bus you're going to have to take.

Do you remember the story of the ancient Greeks about the Minotaur? The Minotaur was a terrible monster that lived deep underground in a labyrinth of caves and passages. And every year the Minotaur devoured young children, ate them up! And someone had to put a stop to it. So young Theseus did the work. He went down into the realms of darkness, and took his sword and braved the beast and slew it dead! But how would he get out? How would he find his way back to the surface? How would he take the right turns and pass through the right gates in this maze? All above him said he was lost. Even though the Minotaur had stopped its fierce bellowing. But one who loved young Theseus didn't give up hope. In fact, she knew she didn't need to. For she had handed Theseus a ball of string. And when he started out, there in the land where he belonged, he tied the end of the string. And when he wanted to return, all that was left for him to do was to follow the string of his love. And it opened for him the right doors. And it took him on the right paths. And it marked for him the right gates. And it led him to the place he knew he must be. It helped him catch the right bus.

And there's the gospel this morning. For all our education, and all our training, and all our decision making is, in some way, following the string that was handed to us by others.

And one time, long ago, when the labyrinth of life around us was roaring with the rough meanness of the

Minotaur, a dying man came into our caves and our dark passages. And he found the beast, and he slew it. And he did one thing more. He handed us a golden string: the way out; the way of life; the ticket on the right bus. Listen to the words of Blake! They're really the words of our Christ. He says to us: "I give you the end of a golden string. Only wind it into a ball, It will lead you in at Heaven's gate, Built in Jerusalem's wall."

Have you found that string? Are you on the right bus in life? And have you brought your young ones along?

A Place at the King's Table
Communion
Jeremiah 52:31-34; Ephesians 2:1-7

This morning the elements of Communion are before us. We've done this so many times. Can it mean something for us again?

Let me give you a picture that will wake you up and shake your head with wonder as you come to the Table today. Imagine the great hall of the kings of Babylon. Here's a room twice the size of this one, columns supporting the roof, spaces off to the sides where servants mysteriously disappear and reappear. Flood this room with tapestries, wall hangings of bright colors contrasted with royal blues and reds. Then fill the air with mixed scents. There's the aroma of perfumes: every time a young female slave passes by she trails behind her the scent of pleasure. And at the edges of the room are the incense pots: cinnamon and jasmine, and cedar scents wafting on the smokes that weave through the room. And then, from beyond the halls at the sides of the room come the smells of food: roasting meats, aromatic spices, the yeasty delight of fresh baked bread. Now imagine a large table, half a circle round, nearly filling this hall. Around it sit the power-brokers of the world. These are the kings of the nations. Once they ruled proudly, passionately, profitably (at least for themselves), over lands and people stretching from India to Greece, from Egypt to the Caspian. Now they're the children of a greater god, the mighty sovereign of Babylon. They still broker power, but now they do it for him. They keep their scattered peoples in line, so that the wealth of the nations pours into this sacred city. And here they sit to feast. All is splendor. All is radiance. All is grandly lavish.

Then the soft sounds of music hush. The drums roll. The kings rise. The servants bow. This is the grand entrance of Amel-Marduk, prince of the world! Crowned with splendor, he sweeps the room with his gaze, and grants his peace. Now he take his place, not at the half-circle table that faces him, but at the King's Table, raised high on a podium, center of attention, seat of prominence. All the other kings in the room look to him. He is their master, their sovereign, their god. He takes his royal seat with benevolent dignity. And suddenly the feasting begins: music mounts up in spritely serenade; dancers explode onto the floor at the center of the half-circle and servants flood the tables with food. And reigning over all his brood, Amel-Marduk smiles.

And then it happens. He beckons his aide to his side. He whispers a command. The aide disappears. A few moments later he returns from the shadows. Arm in arm with another man. And the loud talk in the room hushes. And the musicians forget their tunes. And the dancers freeze like statues. Because the man who enters is a prisoner. Prison rags. Prison dirt. Prison shaggy hair. Prison skin and bones. He stoops from ill health. He wheezes a cough. Thirty-seven years he's been in the pit! His hollow eyes blink at these soft lights! And then the strangest of all things happens. The great Amel-Marduk stands! He stands to greet this miserable wretch! He stands to honor him! He stands to welcome him like an equal! Like a brother! And then he motions the servants to set a place for the man. Where? Among the other kings? At a corner table in the back? On the floor with the festival scraps? No! He takes the man by the arm. And he leads him to a seat at his own high perch! At his own right hand! A place of honor at the king's table!

"In the year Amel-Marduk became king of Babylon, in the thirty-seventh year of the exile of Jehoiachin, king of Judah, Amel-Marduk released Jehoiachin from prison on the 25th day of the 12th month. He spoke kindly to him and gave him a seat of honor higher than those of the other kings who were with him in Babylon. So Jehoiachin put aside his prison clothes and for the rest of his life ate regularly at the king's table." (Jeremiah 52:31-33)

Do you see it?! Then, says the Apostle Paul, you know who you are! Once dead inside, once lost and bewildered, once stuck in the prison of your guilt and your shame and your memories. But God...! But God took you from prison! And He made you alive in Christ! And today He calls you to your place at the King's table!

What's the prison that has held you? Is it some addiction, some cycle of behavior, some callousness or hypocrisy? Come out of it, friend... Come out of it today, and take your place at the King's table! Are you trapped by the memories of the past? Failed relationships? Lost opportunities? I come to you this morning as aide to the King. He opens the door to your cell and calls you to a new future; his future. Come and find your place at the King's table! What restlessness troubles you today? Do you ache for a world that reels in chaos? Do you search for a love that heals? Do you need a new place for your heart to call home? Then come! Come, for the feast is spread!

"Don't Let Me Come Home A Stranger!"
John 15:9-17

What did people do before television? Did you ever think about that? Pastor Peter and I were just at a Church Leaders Conference a week ago, and the speaker said that no one thing in the history of the world has changed the habits of people like the television. We don't want to admit it. But it's probably true for most of us here.

So what did people do before television? Well, I know what some people used to do. They used to go out in the evenings to hear speakers! In fact, you know Mark Twain. He's the fellow that gave us those wonderful stories about Tom Sawyer and Huckleberry Finn. Mark Twain used to be a traveling speaker. He made his living that way for a while. He used to travel all across North America, stopping in little towns along the way, and giving a humorous lecture in the evening. One time he came to a small town, and it was only early in the afternoon. So he went to the general store, and he struck up a conversation with the owner. Say! he said, I'm new in town! What's a feller to do here for a little excitement? Oh! said the proprietor, I expect there's going to be a speaker over at the town hall this evening; people have been coming in here all day to buy up my tomatoes and rotten eggs to throw at the man!

Well, I hope you haven't brought any tomatoes or rotten eggs with you this morning to throw at me. But I do want to share with you something that Mark Twain once said. It's kind of the summary of what this message is all about this morning. He said: "The proper office of a friend is to side with you when you are in the wrong. Nearly anybody will side with you when you are in the right."

That's probably as good a definition of friendship as you'll find anywhere: Somebody who'll be there for you even when you're wrong! A friend doesn't have to agree with you. But a friend...a true friend, will always stick with you. Especially in tough times.

Your list of friends is probably a lot like mine. I've known a lot of people in my short life. And many of them have been my friends. I've known times of great loves and great relationships. And I've known times of great loneliness. Two friends in particular hurt me badly. One was supposedly my best friend when I was a boy. We did everything together for a few years. Then he switched allegiances, and he shut me out of his life. I was only 14 at the time. And I remember the feeling of loss in my life. It was so real, so powerful, so over-whelming! There was anger, on the one hand: How could he do this to me?! Who does he think he is?! I'm never going to talk to him again! But on the other side there was a lot of doubt, and pain, and fear: What's wrong with me?! Why doesn't he like me anymore?! Maybe no one really likes me! And I wondered if anybody would miss me if I'd suddenly die. Maybe not! I could just see it. My family would gather at the breakfast table, and they'd all sit down to eat. And they'd carry on their usual conversations. And my sisters would kick each other under the table. And nobody would even notice that I wasn't there! I could be lying in my bed, stiff and cold, and they wouldn't even realize it! And then, maybe, my baby brother Lyle, sitting in his high chair, would throw his food around. And some would land on my chair. And Mom would clean it up after breakfast. And she'd say to herself, Hmmm! Nobody sat here this morning! And she'd shake her head. And then she'd just turn and walk away. Do you remember feeling like that, when you were younger? Some of you must!

The other friend who hurt me was one of my girlfriends at college. I thought she loved me. She said she loved me. We dated for a little while. We both worked at the same radio station, and I'd come in, early in the morning, and there would be a little note that she left for me, when she signed off the night before. And then, one day, I found out she was teasing me. She was using me to get back at an old boyfriend. She didn't really care about me at all. And I remember how devastated I was. I went to the dorm room of another friend. He could see I wasn't doing so well. He asked me how I was. I didn't say anything. I just went to his stereo. He had this big pile of old records. And I put on that one song that said it all: "Why does the sun go on shining? Why do the birds soar through the sky? Don't they know it's the end of the world? It ended when you said goodbye!" Remember that? Remember when you felt that way?

But there's the other side of it too. I had a good friend during college and seminary. He's still a friend today. When I almost quit seminary, he was there for me. When I went through a dark and deep and dreary depression, he took me in. He fed me meals when I didn't feel like taking care of myself. He took me fishing when I didn't really want to do anything. He held me in the grip of his confidence when I didn't even know who I was myself. That's the kind of friend Mark Twain was talking about.

Why? What's in a friendship for me? (To be myself; to see myself.)

A few years back (1985), Canadian researcher Donald Posterski surveyed nearly 4000 young people across Canada. He asked them what they wanted out of life. He asked them about their values, their goals, their hopes and dreams, their needs. Here's something that might amaze you: only 2 out of 10 said that they wanted to be popular! Can you believe it?! Somehow, in the way we talk to each other, that seems to be so important! Even our young daughters, in grades 1, 2, and 3, come home from school and tell us who's popular and who's not! But no, say young people across Canada! That's really not the most important thing to us! Forty-one percent said that it was really important to them that God accepted them. That's encouraging, I guess. Around half of the people Mr. Posterski surveyed said they were looking for success, or freedom, or a comfortable life. That's what they were aiming for. That's really what they wanted. Sixty-five percent said that family life was very important to them. But here were the two things at the top of the list: Eighty-seven percent said that they could give up everything else in life, if only they knew that they were loved. And over 90 percent said that the highest value in their lives, the thing they needed most, the one thing they couldn't live without was a friend! A friend!

Do you know why! Well, for one thing, people need friends in order to be themselves. That's the way God made us, isn't it? Remember the story of creation? Adam was alone in the world. Sure, he had all the animals to play with, but the gazelles could run faster, and the giraffes could reach higher, and the monkeys were always running off to play their own games. Besides, they didn't talk well with him. So God made Eve. I don't know if you've ever thought about it, but the story of the Bible begins in a garden, where two people had a little picnic together. And then it goes on from there till it ends in the book of Revelation, in a city. In the New Jerusalem. In the world to come, where we'll finally be able to live together in love, and in joy, and in friendship. We can't really be ourselves apart from others.

19

Over the years, scientists have tried these experiments with isolation. They'll put someone in a tank of water, dark, quiet, alone. They'll let that person stay there for a long while, and they'll hook up electrodes, to monitor the pulses of the brain. Invariably, do you know what happens? Invariably those people will begin to dream. They'll start out dreaming about other people, about other times, when they were touched, or held, or when they had good conversation together. Usually they even laugh out loud, just to hear the sound of a voice. Then they'll get depressed. They'll get lonely and depressed. They'll wonder if the scientists have forgotten them. They'll imagine that the world came to an end, and they've been left there forever: isolated, trapped, the living dead. And then, say the scientists, they'll go into hallucinatory nightmares. They'll scream and they'll whimper and they'll beg someone, anyone, to hear them, to touch them, to hold them.

We can't be ourselves till we find ourselves in relation to others. No man is an island, said John Donne. And he was right. I had a friend, years ago, who was going through a tough time in his dating relationship. He wrote a poem about it. This is what he said: "Friends. What are friends for? Friends are for friends. A redundant statement, but true. Someone to share with, both joy and sorrow. Someone to cheer. Someone to comfort. Are you afraid of me? I wish you weren't. If I hurt you I would be hurting myself! If you're afraid of me, I'm afraid of me, too! I could say 'Forget it! Let's not be friends!' But that's what I've been doing for a long time. I want to change. Can we be friends again, if we've ever been Friends? And if we haven't, can we start being Friends?" (John Van Milligan)

We need friends in order to be fully human, fully alive. That's the way God made us. And we need friends in order to see ourselves, too. I've never known as much about myself as I've known through the eyes of my closest friends. They help me see who I am. They help me understand what I'm all about. Some years ago, a grade 12 student in Lethbridge, Alberta, wrote about that. She told of how much she needed her friend in order to find herself. Listen to her words. She calls her poem "Caged Emotions:"

"I've often wondered:
What happens
When your life falls apart
Before your eyes?
Now I know the answer.

Nothing.
Absolutely nothing.
Life goes on.
The birds still sing and
The grass still grows.

Things only change
Inside myself.
I have to find
A new direction in life,
But you never see this.

You see a happy person,
Much contented with life.
Someone who never has doubts,
Or fears, or emotions.
Even though I do.

But no one knows me.
I mean the real me.
The one part of me that

Counts the most.
My doubts and fears and emotions.

These things remain inside.
Locked up like a wild tiger
Who is waiting for
The right moment and person
To open the door and set it free.

I have been waiting for
The right moment and person.
I know that you are
The right person,
But is this the right moment?

Will it ever be?
The right moment, I mean.
You're so entwined
In your world
You have no time for mine.

I wish with all my heart
That you could find time for me
And unlock my cage
At the right time.
When we are both ready.

I think we are both ready.
I know I am.
But I want you
To be too.
I hope you are ready soon.

Because if you are not
I will attempt to flee my cage

At the wrong moment.
And I will be shot down
Because of my impatience.

And in my last moments
You won't see me
As secure
And independent.

You'll see someone
Who has doubts
And deep fears
And emotions.
And then I'll wonder;
Is that really so bad?" (Renita Klassen)

We need friends because that's the way God made us. And we need friends in order to truly be ourselves. And we need friends in order to truly see ourselves.

Where can I find true friendship? (In giving; in grace)

So where do we find friends these days? Jesus tells us here in these few verses. He tells us two things. First, he tells us that we find friendship in giving. In giving ourselves to others. "Greater love has no one than this, that he lay down his life for his friends."

Isn't that what Jesus' testimony is all about? Friendship begins in giving. No one who long grasps tightly to himself, no one who lives always deeply withdrawn into herself, will understand what friendship is all about. Friendship comes in giving, not getting. One speaker remembers standing in front of a crowd during a Singles Retreat weekend. And a woman rose to challenge him. She didn't like what he was saying. Look at me! she said. I'm fat and ugly! My husband left me for his pretty young secretary! I'm broke! I can't get a job! I've got four kids to feed! And my nerves are shot, so I chain smoke! Who'll be my friend?! Nobody wants me! The speaker says he was taken aback. What could he say to her? What would you say? Slowly he drew her out: how was she feeling? What was she thinking? Why did she say that? And slowly her sad story unfolded. And then he did something he never even expected of himself. He says it just came to him, kind of like a whispering within. He said to her: Give what you need! She said: What?! He said: You've got to give what you need! She said: What do you mean: Give what I need?! What kind of crazy advice is that?! He said: Well, look at it this way: What do you need most in your life? She said: I need someone to tell me I'm still okay! He said: What else?! She said: I need someone to listen to me! I'm so tired of being alone! He said: What else?! She said: I need someone to take the kids once in a while. I need to get out of the house and find myself again. He said: What else?! She said: I need to eat better, and get things cleaned up at home. He said: What else?! She said: Isn't that enough?! He said: Give what you need! He said: Do you know anybody else who needs those things! Yeah! She said, I believe I do! He said: Give that person what you need most in life! And that was that. She sat down, again, thoughtful. And he forgot all about it. Until 18 months later. When a woman came up to him in another place. And she said: Remember me?! And he didn't. And she said: You told me to give what I need, remember?! And then he did. And she said: I didn't know life could be so good!

Friendship, said Samuel Taylor Coleridge, is a sheltering tree... And that it is. And those who find it are usually those who give it.

But here's the strange thing. Many of us can't give it: we've been hurt too deeply. And many of us can't give it: because we're still too caught up in our own selves even to begin to reach out to someone else. Many of us just can't find it in ourselves to give and to give and to give.

And that's where the gospel brings us this morning. To Jesus. To grace. To the One who said: I came that you might have life abundantly. To the One who said: As the Father has loved me, so I have loved you. To the One who said: I am the vine, and you are the branches. Find your life in me!

Joseph Scriven did that. He was born near the beginning of the last century in Dublin, Ireland. Life was rather normal for him. He went to school. He went on to college. He had the usual set of friends and buddies. And then he even met the woman of his dreams. They were engaged to be married. The night before the wedding something happened. She died suddenly, drowned in the waters of a river she was crossing. Joseph was devastated. He didn't know what to do with himself. His best friend was gone. And his life disappeared with her. For a while he moped about in despair. Then he bought passage on a ship to Canada. He settled here in Ontario, near Port Hope. And for a while he lingered on in his grief and sorrow. Till eventually life carried him on ahead, and he picked up whatever pieces he could. Then came the news. His mother was ill. She wasn't expected to live. And that night he sat at his desk, thinking about all he'd gone through himself, and wishing he could be there for his mother. He spent some time in prayer. And then he wrote a little poem. He sent it to her the next day. Thankfully, his mother recovered, and lived a good, long life.

But then it happened. One day her neighbor took sick. And she felt the anguish of soul that comes to those who care. And, being a woman of few words, she did only two things: she slipped over to her neighbor's house with some good cooking; and she pressed into her neighbor's palm the little verses written by her son those years before. Otherwise we might never have come to know, and to love, and to sing these wonderful words of Joseph Scriven:

"What a friend we have in Jesus, all our sins and grief to bear! What a privilege to carry everything to God in prayer! Oh, what peace we often forfeit! Oh, what needless pain we bear! All because we do not carry everything to God in prayer!

"Can we find a friend so faithful who will all our sorrows share? Jesus knows our every weakness; take it to the Lord in prayer. Do your friends despise, forsake you? Take it to the Lord in prayer. In his arms he'll take and shield you; you will find a solace there."

Who are you this morning? In a sense, you are your friends! In them you find yourself completed. And in them you find yourself mirrored, so that you truly learn who you are. And when it comes to friend-making, it happens through giving and it happens through grace. It happens when we give to others what we ourselves need in life. And it happens when, even after the giving stops, we find ourselves drawn toward heaven, in the grace, and in the love, and in the caring, and in the friendship of our Lord Jesus. How did John put it? We love, because he first loved us!

Maybe you know that this morning. Then I hope you don't mind the reminders I've given you. But maybe you don't know that this morning. I remember how it was for me in May 1986. We had spent the year in Nigeria, and then we had to come suddenly back to

Canada, because of medical reasons. And I left Brenda and the girls with Brenda's parents in Alberta. I flew back to Nigeria to finish my work. And those were nine of the loneliest weeks of my life. And one night, when I was listening to my short wave radio, I heard a song that became the cry of my heart. The first part was all about friends and family. It went like this: "As I walked out one evening to breathe the air and soothe my mind,/ I thought of friends and the home I had/And all the things I'd left behind./Will there come a time when the memories fade/And pass on with the long, long years?/When ties no longer bind?/Lord, save me from this darkest fear:/Don't let me come home a stranger!/I couldn't stand to be a stranger!" And in my mind's eye I pictured Brenda, and Kristyn and Kimberly and Kaitlyn.... And my prayer was the prayer of that song: Lord, help them to remember me! Don't let me come home a stranger! I couldn't stand it! And then the song went on. And it made a marvelous turn. It set those same thoughts in a global perspective. And it prayed this prayer: "And as I walk this universe,/I free my mind of time and space. I wander through the galaxies/But never do I find my place./Will there come a time when the memories fade/And pass on with the long, long years?/When the ties no longer bind?/Lord, save me from this darkest fear:/Don't let me come home a stranger!/I couldn't stand to be a stranger!"

Do you ever sing that song? Do you ever think about those things? Do you ever pray: Lord, when time has run its course, when my little life is over, when eternity calls me away from earth, don't let me come home a stranger! If you do, then may you find the answer to your question in the friendship of Jesus! And may you find him in the ministries of this church!

Dreamers
Pentecost
Acts 2

This is Pentecost Sunday. You know what it's about, don't you? Pentecost was one of the three "High Holidays" of the Jewish people. There was the Day of Atonement, when they took the lamb and they slaughtered it and they brought its blood into the Holy of Holies at the heart of the Temple, and they cried out to God to forgive their sins, their individual sins, their personal sins, their national sins, the sins of their leaders, the sins they did and were ashamed of, and the sins they didn't even know about, the sins that happened when they chose to do the wrong thing, and the sins that happened when they didn't do anything at all, and a child died, or a widow suffered, or a neighbor had to sell his farm...That's what the Day of Atonement was all about. Then there was the Passover. That was the day for memories: Remember when our people were slaves in Egypt? Remember the great plagues of God on Pharaoh? Remember that little man Moses, and how God shook Egypt through him? And remember the night of all nights, the night of the Angel of Death, the night of the guardian blood of the lamb, the night of the quick meal, of the hurried packing, of the bread not yet risen?! Remember? Remember? Do you remember what God did for us? Do you know who you are?!

But today is Pentecost. This is the third of the great Jewish High Holidays. It's 50 days after the Passover. That's why they named it Pentecost---fifty days. That's not its real name, of course. The real name of this great celebration is "Firstfruits." The Feast of the Firstfruits. Do you know what people did on this day? You don't really read about it in Acts chapter 2. You just hear

28

that there were a lot of people visiting Jerusalem, Jews from nations all over the world. What were they doing? Well, in Palestine at this time of the year, the growing season is just about over. The crops are hanging heavy in the field and in the vineyards. You can see the whiteness of the wheatfields. You can search among the leaves and gather great bunches of grapes. You can taste all the new olives on the tree. But before any harvesting could happen, Jewish people around the world did one very important thing. They took just a sample of the grains, and just a few clusters of grapes, and just one or two of the first lambs in the new flock, and just a small jar of the first pressings of olive oil. And they brought these to Jerusalem. To the Temple. And they carried them into the Temple courts, and they laid them on the altars there, to be burned to God as a sacrifice or to be given to the poor and homeless. And then they would have a party. And that party would last several days. The musicians would set themselves up in the Temple Courts. And the men would dance around, and they would sing Psalms 113 to 120. And the wine would flow. And the people would get drunk. And everybody would have a good time. And what was the point of it all? Well, it was this: The Harvest belonged to the Lord! The Harvest belonged to the Lord! The farmer may have sowed the seed, but God made it grow. The vinedresser may have pruned the vines, but God gave the grapes. The stockman may have culled the herd, but it was God who brought the tiny little lambs and calves and foals from their mothers' wombs into the wide expanses of this world. And the Feast of Firstfruits is their way of saying, Thank you! Thank you, God! Thanks for taking care of us! Thanks for your creation! Thanks for placing us in this wonderfully complex, this teeming, alive world! Thank you, God! And no one would even think of going home to the harvest until first they had stopped for these days in Jerusalem.

And now you know the rest of the story. Why did Jesus tell his followers to wait? Why did they stay there in Jerusalem, all huddled together, when there was so much they could have done? Just for this reason: Pentecost was coming! The Feast of Firstfruits was just around the corner! And on this day, by the power of the Holy Spirit, the great harvest of heaven would begin! The great mission harvest of the church had to wait until Pentecost. Now God will bring in His harvest. On this day, the firstfruits, the first 3000 new Christians. And once the festival days are ended, the workers will go out to the rest of the harvestfields of the world. And then the great mission harvest of the Church would begin. Just wait! said Jesus. You'll know the right time when it comes! And so they did.

And that brings us to our text this morning. Because here Peter stands up, and he paints a picture for the crowds. Peter says those who are part of the Harvest of Heaven are dreamers. He calls them dreamers. He calls me a dreamer, I suppose. Maybe he's calling you a dreamer. I hope so. And he does that when he quotes the old prophecy of Joel from centuries before. God's going to do an amazing thing one day, says Joel. And when it happens, look for the dreamers!

Now, sometimes we don't want to be called a dreamer, do we?! I remember a fellow who was in my class at school, and our teachers always called him a dreamer. They were kind. I won't tell you what the rest of us called him. But you know him, if I tell you about him. Because you've met him along the way yourself. Always in a world of his own. Eyes in a distant focus. Head on his hand as he sat at his desk. He stumbled when he walked, because he didn't look where he was going.

Absent-minded. You know him, don't you? Space ca-
dets! we sometimes say. Earth calling Charlie! Earth
calling Charlie! Come in, Charlie! But Charlie would sit
there in his dream-world. And we don't really want to
be like that, do we?!

Or sometimes we meet people, and their dreams
are too fantastic. We don't want to be like them, either,
because their ideas are always a little strange. There was
a man who used to stop by my study when I was working
at a church in Anchorage, Alaska. And I really disliked
it when he came. Because he could only talk about two
things. For one thing, he talked about a Christian radio
station. That was one of his hopes and dreams and goals.
He was always going to set up a Christian radio station
there in Anchorage. But the problem was that he only
talked his dream. And he never did anything about it.
Talk, talk, talk. And then he'd suddenly stop, and he'd
get down on his knees, and he'd tell me to pray for him.
He'd even put my hand on his head! And now I had to
pray for him and for his radio station. But he didn't do a
thing about it. His dream was all talk. I told you that he
only talked to me about two things. One was his dream
of a Christian radio station. Here's the other. There was
one cloverleaf interchange on the main highway coming
into Anchorage. And there were four tall light-poles
there to light it at night. And, according to this fellow,
those were the tallest light-poles in the world. He'd
gotten that information somewhere. Anyway, he had a
personal plan for those light-poles. One day soon, he
said, he was going to strap on his mountain climbing
gear, and he was going to climb one of those tall light
poles for the Lord. That was his dream. And nobody
really wanted to be like him. Nobody shared his fanciful
dreams. A United Methodist bishop (John Wesley
Hardt) tells of the time that he visited a woman in a

retirement home. She was one hundred years old! And they gave her a party! And she was surrounded by friends and festivities. And Bishop Hardt loved the woman. And while he was sitting there with her, a reporter came by from the local newspaper. He wanted a story for the gossip page. Do you have any children? he asked her. And she looked at him with a twinkle in her eye, and she said: Not yet! Now, that's dreaming!

But who are these dreamers of Pentecost, these dreamers of Joel and of Peter, these dreamers of the Harvest of Heaven?! Well, we can say several things about them.

For one thing, they know their history. If you read Peter's whole speech that day, you'll soon realize this about it: he doesn't say anything new! He doesn't say anything new! Everything he says is a history lesson! God did this! The prophets said that! This is what happened to Jesus! Here's what you were doing! It's all history! Peter and the others weren't dreamers because they suddenly flipped out, because they suddenly became glassy-eyed and useless. They were dreamers in the Harvest of Heaven because they knew their history, and they knew what God was doing all along.

Real dreams are like that, aren't they?! Everybody dreams when they sleep. Did you know that? You dream, even if you never remember your dreams. Kaitlyn, our youngest, came to us with her latest dream this week. She said that in her dream she was talking with Mommy, and Mommy was walking around the bed in her room, and the further Mommy walked, the more she shrank, until she became just a key lying on the floor. We've been sitting up nights ever since, trying to figure that one out! But everybody dreams. An average of 4 to 6 dreams a night! And here's the thing about our dreams: We can never have a dream which is not couched in terms and in pictures and involving people except for those things that we have personally experienced for ourselves during our waking hours! Our dreams may change what we've experienced. And we may learn new things from what we've experienced. But every detail in our dreams will be something that we are otherwise very familiar with. They say that when the German chemist Von Stradonitz was working to find the formula for benzene, it just wouldn't come to him. He made his calculations over and over again, but it never came out right. And then one day he was on a bus. And he was tired. And his eyelids sagged. And his body slouched. And he entered that twilight world, half-way between the conscious and the unconscious. And then he saw it. With his mind? With his eye? In a dream? Who knows?! He saw atoms dancing in front of his face in a whirl. And then he saw things like snakes slipping round them and joining one end to the other. And Von Stradonitz thought they looked a lot like the symbols of the ancient alchemists that he'd studied: snakes biting their tails. And when he got back to his laboratory, he thought about those images, and he wrote down a formula that used those ideas, and he created the chemical description of benzene. All because of a dream.

But here's the thing: his dream came from the things he already knew, from the things that he had studied, from the lessons of history. And that's the truth of dreams. And that's the truth of faith as well. Some people only want the experience of God. The "Pentecostal" experience, they call it. The excitement, the sensation, the burning of the moment. But don't think it means much if you don't know your history! You can't understand the dreams of God by looking at only a single event! Only by looking backward can you begin to find His plans and His purposes. Kierkegaard said: We must live our lives forward, but they can only be understood backward. And this is a lesson we need to learn over and over again. Some Christians demand a daily miracle in order to believe. Do this for me, God! they say. Make that happen for my family! And if God doesn't provide it, they threaten to stop believing in Him! All their spiritual expectations must be gratified right now! But if you live like that, if you want a faith like that, then there are some deep lessons of life that God can never teach you. That's why the poet Robert Frost wrote a poem about Job. You know, the book of Job in the old Testament. Where Job goes through all that suffering. Actually, Frost's poem is about God. In fact, he gave it this title.

He called it: "God's Thanks to Job." And it's all about God thanking Job for hanging in there, for believing, even through his pain. God says, in Robert Frost's poem: "Used to be I have to reward them all instantly; But you've changed all that!"

But some of us haven't learned that lesson yet. If you think that all you have to do is pray for an empty parking spot when you go shopping downtown, and God's going to give it to you, then there are some lessons of faith that you'll never learn. Faith isn't something that you get in bunches, and then you have it confirmed day by day and hour by hour every time you put God to the test. Can you imagine doing that to your friend? Can you imagine saying to her: Well, you can be my friend, and I will trust you, as long as you persuade me, every moment, that you are worthy of my trust. If you do that very long, I can tell you that you won't have many friends! Good friends are good friends because they have a history together! And even when, in this instant, it seems that I should mistrust you, I know, from our times together, what you're all about! And I will stick close to you, and I will love you, and I will dream your dreams with you, because I know your history!

Remember the experience that C. S. Lewis had? Once he became a Christian he grew to have a deep and steady and profound devotion to his Lord. And then his wife died. His wife named Joy. The Joy of his life. And C. S. Lewis kept a journal of his thoughts. And you can find them today on the shelves of most good bookstores. It's his little book called *A Grief Observed*. And what will you read there? Will you read that God comforted him, that God was close to him, that God was the source of his strength?! You will not!!! You'll find instead the cry of loneliness! You'll find the heartbreak of despair! You'll find Lewis shouting his prayers to God. "But," says Lewis, "I hear the bolts of heaven sliding into their slots, and the gates of mercy are sealed up tight, and the skies above become a hard sheet of polished brass!" That's what Lewis writes. But then keep reading. Because Lewis takes his time. He takes two years of time. And he reflects on history. And slowly he comes round to this: that there are treasures of darkness as well as treasures of light. That God is not at our disposal, but that we are at His. That even the experience of the absence of God, is still the experience of God. And that there are lessons of life and of faith and of mercy to be learned even in our darkest hours.

Now, let's get back to Pentecost. What's at stake in the dreamers of the harvest of heaven? Isn't it this: that they know enough history of God and of His kingdom that they understand what He's up to, what His purposes are, what His character is like, even when the present circumstances of life are a maze and a muddle and a mixer-bowl of conflicting news reports! Why do we have the Bible? Why does the church thrive on history? Do you know that history becomes important in every civilization touched by Christianity? And it's for this reason: those who would become the Dreamers of Pentecost live in the context of God's history! Do you realize what it was that the church did to you the day you were baptized? Think of it! Here's the story of Pentecost. And at the end of Peter's sermon, 3000 people are going to shout: What do we do now?! And Peter is going to tell them: Believe this message! And then be baptized! Why be baptized?! What's the significance! Do you know? It's this: when you are baptized, you are taken into the history of the Covenant of Grace! You are given a past that makes sense. It's the past of what God has been doing all along, since He gathered Adam into His arms, since He spoke to Abraham, since He led His people Israel through the deserts, since He filled the hearts of the Psalmists with their songs, since He marched through the wilderness with the Exiles, since He entered the world as a baby in Bethlehem, and cried in pain from the cross of Calvary... And now it's all yours! This is who you really are! Not just an experience, but a history! Not just a moment, but a heritage! Not just an explosion of miracles, but a deep and true and profound walk of friendship with God. And then you start to dream. And then you know who you are. And then you see the vision of God's ways and God's work in God's world.

That's the first thing this morning. The dreamers of the harvest of Heaven know their history. And here's the second thing, and this is really all I'll mention today. **The dreamers that Peter and Joel talk about choose to do good.** Think of it! Here's Peter, standing before a crowd of people, many of whom only 52 days earlier had shouted for the death of Jesus. And now he was preaching Jesus! And what a strange thing it must have been for him! He wanted to run away and hide! He wanted to go back to Galilee, and jump into a fishing boat! Jerusalem became, to him, a strange and alien place, with enemies all around. And this too: there was a time when he wanted to repay evil for evil. He wanted to kill these people! He wanted to take out his sword and slash them limb from limb! And now to stand in front of this crowd that spit on Jesus was a very strange thing for him. And here's the stranger thing: He stirs up that very hornets' nest again! He says to these people: You put him to death! You killed him! What does he want? A riot? Remember the race riots of the past months? Isn't that what Peter is stirring up?! One might think so! But here's the difference: Peter says that God took that bloody murder, and He made it part of His larger plans. God took the evil, and He turned it to good. And those who dream the dreams of heaven do the same thing. Peter stands here not to hate this crowd, not to dig in the wounds that are festering, not to add insult to injury. He stands here now filled with the power and the love of God. Where evil ruled, Peter breathes the Spirit of the Love of God. Peter doesn't explain evil. But he says that good can come out of it.

Some talk to Mother Teresa in Calcutta. And they ask her if she understands the problems of evil and of suffering. How could a good God allow these kinds of things to happen? Why do the children die? You know the questions. And do you know what she says? She says: I don't understand these things! Of course I don't understand them! Who does?! But do you know what I do understand? I understand that these little ones die one at a time, and I understand that I can save them one at a time! And so she does!

Here's where the church gets its mission. Its Pentecostal mission. Because those who dream the dreams of the harvest of Heaven know that God never explains evil for us. He just brings a good out of it. Remember the time that the disciples came to Jesus? They showed him a man who was blind. Blind from birth. Never saw a flower in his life. Never took in a sunset, or watched the way of the eagle on the high currents of the heavens. Never gazed into his mother's eye. Now, they said to Jesus, since you seem to know so much about God, tell us who sinned, so that God did this to him. Was it his parents? Was it his grandparents? Or was it something in his own little heart, even while it was beating in his mother's womb? And do you remember what Jesus did? How he told them they didn't know what they were asking?! And then how he healed the man and gave him his sight?! We focus on the calamity. We try to read the fault, the blame, the sin. But not so Jesus. He healed the man! Healing is always better than explanation!

Where do you find the Holy Spirit of God today? Not in communities that are pointing fingers! Not in hearts that are placing blame! Not in lives that are finding fault! You find the Holy Spirit of God wherever there is healing taking place. That's where the dream of God lives on!

Some years ago, Dr. Leslie Hunter spoke of a dream he'd had. He said that he dreamed that he entered a huge room. It was bright with light, and warm with a kind of coziness that you feel when you go someplace where you're wanted and noticed and loved. And in his dream, he said, he understood what this room was. It was the storage room for all the great gifts of God! Everything good that God had ever given had first been kept here! And he saw an angel at the counter. And he glided over to the angel. (Did you ever notice, in your dreams, how you never really walk or run? It's always more of a glide!) Anyway, he went over to the angel at the counter. And he said to the angel: I've just run out of the Fruit of the Spirit! (You know them from Galatians 5:22--Love, joy, peace, patience, kindness, goodness, faithfulness, gentleness, self-control.) I've just run out of the Fruit of the Spirit! he said to the angel. Can you restock me?! But the angel shook his head. And then Dr. Hunter got angry. And in his dream he shouted: Listen! There's so much fighting, and injustice, and lying, and bitterness in my world, and I need the Fruit of the Spirit! I need it all: Love, Joy, Peace, Patience, Kindness.... If you don't give them to me, I'll be lost! And then, in his dream, says Dr. Hunter, the angel behind the counter said this. He said: We don't stock the Fruit of the Spirit here; we only stock the seed. Would you like that?

Do you see what he's saying? Do you know the meaning of the dream? It's just this: Those who dream the dreams of heaven, those who find the power of Pentecost, those who enter this great harvest field of God, have this sense of purpose. They choose to bring good to their worlds, as God has chosen the same. And it isn't always easy, and it doesn't happen all at once. Sometimes the best you can do is scatter a few seeds of mercy. But that's where the dreams begin. That's where God's dream began: when He planted eternity in your heart. And in the life of Jesus. Wicked people conspired against him: Caiaphas, Herod, Pilate, Judas... But God turned the cruel cross into the good by which we are saved!

That's what it means to be Pentecostal Dreamers! Not just words and words and words with no action. Not just the right theology formed in the right creeds and confession. Not just the self-righteousness that takes pride in itself. It's this: to do justice, to love mercy, and to walk humbly with our God. Do you want to know whether the Holy Spirit of God lives in you? Then ask your spouse or your teenager or your best friend how they see you dealing with evil and with pain and with suffering. Those who dream the dreams of the harvest of Heaven choose to do good, choose to bring good into evil situations, choose to sow the seeds of God's great love.

Sometimes people ask me to explain the Holy Spirit. What is the Holy Spirit? they ask me. God the Father I can understand... Jesus I can understand... But what is the Holy Spirit? And I have to tell them that I don't really know. Because you can't explain the spirit. That's what Jesus himself said to Nicodemus one night. Do you remember? He said that the Spirit is like the wind in the trees: you can't see it... you can't hold it in your hand... you can't order it around... But this you can do: you can know that the Spirit of God is there, when you see what happens in people's lives!

Says the prophet Joel: They turn into dreamers! Says Peter on Pentecost Sunday: We're all dreamers! And that's what the best of the Holy Spirit is all about! The Spirit of God made me a dreamer! He gave me a place in the history of God. And He placed this desire in my heart: to choose to bring the good in all circumstances of life. That's where the dreams of heaven begin!

Taming the Beast
Genesis 4:1-16

Remember the story a couple of years ago? Two high school girls in California, friends,... Both well liked... Both talented and ambitious... Both at center stage in their school's social activities. They came out to the cheerleading tryouts together in their last year. It was a friendly rivalry. But one was selected, and the other didn't make it. And that night a beast came lurking out of the darkness. And he bit the heart of the loser. And she felt the poison charge through her system. And her eyes grew dark and blazing. And her hand found a gun. And her legs stalked their prey. And in the morning, the winner was a loser, and the loser was a devil, and the community choked in pain.

I remember hearing that story for the first time on the radio. The announcer was shocked. I could tell it in his voice. I was shocked. Everyone I talked to was shocked. A lot of news stories are about people far away, and places very distant, and social figures who loom high above us. But here was the girl next door. We saw her on the street. We chatted with her on the bus. We sat next to her at the ball game. She wasn't a strange, cruel stock character in some seedy, B-rated movie. She was our daughter, our sister, ourself. That's why we were shocked.

But the shock was more than just disbelief. The shock was like a revelation. Here was someone who actually did what most of us have felt, now and again. Raging envy. Insane jealousy. How did the cartoonist put it, years ago? He drew a little circle above someone's head, and an arrow pointing to her skull, and then he wrote the truth of the matter: Urge to kill!

The story is so real because the beast lurks in every human heart. Did it ever strike you that one of the first news stories in the Bible is this story played over again in its first version: Cain and Abel are brothers. They romped together in the dirt as kids. They built their forts, and they carved their initials in the trunks of trees. They swam in the river, and they ran races against the animals and against each other. They were brothers and rivals and friends. They even worshipped together. Adam and Eve showed them the way. They told the boys about the early days, about the days when they walked and talked together in the Garden with God. They showed Abel and Cain how to build a sacrifice. Because God stayed a little ways away now, and they had to talk to him through smoke signals. And they build their altars, and they arrange their prayers, and they strike up the song of the fire, and they send their praise and thanks to God. And then comes the word from heaven: Abel makes the cheerleading team, but Cain is cut from the roster.

Why? Why, why, why?! I remember hearing this story as a little boy, and feeling so sorry for Cain. Didn't he get shafted by God? Didn't he bring an offering too? Why should God pick favorites? I grew up on the edges of the social fringe. I knew what it was like to be passed by. When they chose teams for baseball at the church picnic, my name was one of the last ones called. And the team captain who finally mumbled for me to come over was more embarrassed for me than anything else. I could feel Cain's pain. No matter what he does, it's never good enough!

We don't know how Cain knew the judgment against him. Maybe, like they used to picture in our Bible Story books, the smoke from Abel's sacrifice zoomed straight up, caught in the wind-tunnel of grace.

And maybe the flames under Cain's offering sputtered and sizzled, and the smoke clouded around like a back-yard barbecue. Maybe Cain kept records of the next six months, and his fields went rancid, while Abel's flocks exploded. I don't know how he knew. But he knew. He knew like I knew, back there in Bunde, Minnesota. He knew like all those who are passed by know. Someone else wins, and I'm a loser.

And that's the jungle where the beast lurks. Gore Vidal, the historian, says: Every time a friend succeeds, I die a little. He knows what it's like in the jungle.

I think there are three major paths though the jungle of the beast, and I want to spend a little time mapping out each this morning. Cain lives in your soul, like he lives in mine. But we only see him when we're walking certain paths.

One of those paths is the path of the Achiever. The path of the Lone Ranger. The path of the Rugged Individualist. The path of the "I Did It My Way" Person. Good stuff, where we can make it on our own. But the problem comes when another Achiever makes it on his own. And he does it on our turf, in our own backyard. Last week five of us were at Willow Creek Community Church, on the northwest side of Chicago. And you can't believe the size of that place until you see it for yourself. It's larger than any of the malls here in London! Really! One church! A congregation of 17,000! 20,000 people coming to worship on the weekend! And the main pastor is good! He's real good! And we sit together. And we hear what they've been able to do there, by the grace of God, and people say: Now that's preaching! And they say: What a leader! And they look around and they say: I wish I could be part of this church! And all the while I'm dancing around them, and pointing fingers at myself, and trying to get them to look at me! You bet I'm envious! I'm so jealous I can taste it!

And you can't often make me jealous. I'm not what you would call a very envious person. When you succeed in business, I'm happy for you! When you do well at school, I think it's wonderful! Even in sports... I've gotten past my old hurts there. The Blue Jays haven't called me up yet, and asked me to come out to the game tonight! But I don't really mind! Honestly! I know I'll never be a great athlete. So I'm not really bothered if you are. (Just don't taunt me about my body, okay!)

But I think I know what I'm pretty good at. I think I'm a good pastor. And I think I'm a good preacher and teacher and writer. And I think I've been able to make my way in my fields by doing it my way, by functioning out of my strengths, and my gifts, and my talents. And I want to do well. For God! For my family! For myself! I'm an Achiever. I'll admit it! So you can praise a politician, and I'll agree with you. And you can applaud a musician, and I'll share your enthusiasm. And you can speak highly of a nurse, and I'll be the first to shake her hand. But when you praise another preacher, instinctively I'll try to find every reason in the book to prove you wrong. Why? Because Cain lives inside of me. Because when we walk down that path in the jungle, the path of the Achiever, the path of the Lone Ranger, I've got to own that path. You know, like that bumper sticker that says: Well, as a matter of fact, I do own the road! And everything you give to someone else, you take from me! Right?!

Now, let's be clear here. I'm only exaggerating a little bit. I remember how I struggled with that in my first years as a pastor. Iron Springs, Alberta. Small congregation. They'd had new pastors every four or five years. A lot of great pastors started out in Iron Springs, and there were two in particular. I heard about them all the time. You see, they believed in the Holy Trinity there in Iron Springs. There was God the Father on the throne of heaven. And there was old Rev. John DeJong, standing at his right hand. And there was Rev. Ralph Koops, sitting at his feet. And try as I might, I could never be as good as them! They loved more, and they preached better, and they made more visits, and they helped more people, and they were kinder and better pastors than anyone ever had a right to be! And I envied them. I walked the path of the Lone Ranger. I wanted people to see me, to need me, to love me, to stand in awe of my gifts and talents. I wanted them to look at me, and not at someone else.

Am I alone in this? I don't think so. I think maybe you know what I'm talking about.

There's a second path in the jungle where the beast of envy lurks. **It's the path of the short cut.** It's the path where we think we can get ahead by cutting corners.

That's the reality of this story in Genesis. Why didn't God receive with thanks the sacrifice that Cain brought?! Because Cain took a shortcut! Abel, we're told, brought lambs from his flock that were choice animals. They would have brought top dollar on the market. Abel worshipped God from his heart. He knew worship meant nothing if it didn't mean everything. That's the tragedy of adultery, you know. We have the capacity to love many people in our lives here. But when we speak our vows of marriage, we say that there's something so special about this particular relationship, that it can't and it won't tolerate shared intimacy. I can love many friends. But I can worship only Brenda in my relationships here. She's the only one I can hold in the heart of my heart at one time. And if I try to tuck someone else in there for a moment or an hour or a night, she knows it. She feels it. And so do I. That's the "all-or-nothing"-ness of marriage. And so it is with worship.

Nobody has to worship God, at least not by way of coercion. So I'm always more at home among honest atheists than I am among dishonest church people. You can seek and you can struggle and you can question and you can doubt. But don't play God for the fool. When you walk the path of shortcuts, spiritual or otherwise, the beast of envy looms large.

Remember that best-selling book some years ago: *When Bad Things Happen to Good People*? Jewish Rabbi Harold Kushner wrote it. It sold millions and millions. Well, recently I read a story about a psychologist who went into a deep depression about it. It seems that this fellow was writing a similar book at the time. Kushner's book came out first. And it got the praise. And it sold more than the other guy's book. And people talked about it more. And things got so messed up in the psychologist's head that he went to another psychologist for treatment. And they talked about his envy. Every time Kushner was on television being interviewed about his book, the other fellow went mad with jealousy. He couldn't stand it! Why should Kushner be praised and not him?! Why should Kushner's book sell so well and his so poorly?! And the counselor tried to help him sort it all out, to get it in perspective, to bring things back in line. And here's what they discovered. They found that the man really knew that Kushner's book was better than his. Why? You know why. It's because Harold Kushner and his wife had a son with *progeria*. It's the disease that makes a person age rapidly. The boy was only 9, and he looked like he was fifty. He lost his hair. His skin wrinkled up. His bones got brittle. And he died early in his teen years. And here's his parents. They don't know what to do, how to feel, how to cope. How much suffering can a family stand?! How much suffering can parents watch in their children?! What's the meaning of it all?!

And so Kushner sits down at his desk. And he starts writing. He writes with tears in his eyes, and with a knife in his chest, and with stones of heaviness in his heart. He writes about suffering, and his tears blot the ink and puff the pages. He writes about suffering as a sufferer. And people know it. He's not a doctor reading a chart to them. He's a hurt and bruised and tormented man. And when he writes about suffering, they listen. Because he knows suffering in his own soul.

But what of the other guy? He wanted to write a great book on suffering without going through the pain himself. He wanted to tell people what suffering was all about without feeling the aching of his own heart. He wanted to give people the gift of healing when he didn't even know the disease firsthand. And they turned away, and they went to Kushner, and they sat at his feet. And envy sank its fangs into the writer's soul.

Envy lurks on every shortcut we make in life. Because we want to get something that someone else is getting, but we don't want to do the things they've done for it. Abel didn't earn God's favor with his sacrifice! Sure, God was pleased with it. After all, it came from a heart of devotion. But what Cain tried to do was take a shortcut: he tried to catch the wave without riding the board! I've seen it so often at university. I've been a teaching assistant at Calvin Seminary, and I've taught a class at Redeemer College. And I mark the exams, and invariably a student will come back with envy in his eyes, and with two papers in his hands. One is his own. The other belongs to the student who got an A. And he'll put them side by side, and he'll say, What's the difference?! Why did you score me lower than him?! And the answers they gave may sound similar, but there's a quality about the one that rings true, and there's a quality about the other that breathes of corner-cutting. That whispers of cramming. That shouts of facts without figures. You know what I'm talking about.

It happens everywhere in society. Where people cut corners, chances are there's envy lurking around. You see, corner cutters aren't interested in the task, or the learning, or the career. They're interested in the fame and the acclaim. And they envy those who have it. Do you know anyone there, on the short-cut in your profession? Look into the shadows; you'll find the beast.

There's a third path in the jungle of life where the beast of envy lurks. **It's on the path of the Crushed Spirit.** Why? Because life isn't fair. And there are times when we don't cut any corners, and there are times when we aren't prima donnas, trying to flitter around in the spotlight, but we still cry: FOUL! And we still look with envious eyes at others.

Remember the story of Mozart's life that was told from the perspective of Antonio Salieri? The play and the film were both called *Amadeus*. Salieri was the court musician in Vienna. And he had a right to be. He worked hard at his craft, writing melodies that were nice, and choral pieces that were good, and instrumental works that were fine. He knew that God had blessed him. After all, he was a devout Christian. As a young man he had prayed fervently to God. Just let me make music that will glorify you, Father! Just let me lift the hearts of people to heaven! Just let me serve you through my music! And then came young Mozart, the boy wonder. The child prodigy. He dazzled the crowds, playing at music like it was second nature to him: fingers dancing at the keyboard, melodies complex and fun at the same time, songs that soared till heaven came alive on earth! And here's the catch. Mozart was such an obvious sinner! He was immature, he was vulgar, he was obscene, and he made off with the ladies time and again! And Salieri grew green with envy. How could life be so unfair?! He was the servant of God! Why should Mozart be blessed with such talents?! He lived a life that was pious and obedient! Why should Mozart traffic in only worldly pleasures?! He was the one who spent a lifetime of hard work at this! Why should it all come so easily to Mozart, and at such a young age?! And so the story goes. Until Mozart dies a mysterious death. And Salieri's eyes gleam vengefully. And in the dramatic climax Salieri sits in an insane asylum, and he curses God for denying him the kind of talent that God blessed Mozart with.

Envy lurks on the path of the Crushed Spirit. Why should your marriage end in divorce, while his survives? Why should your business falter in the recession, while hers only grows? Why should your life be plagued with sickness, while his seems never troubled? Remember the two women who came to Solomon that day? One baby between two mothers? He's mine! says the one. No! He's mine! says the other. One baby died, and now both women claim him. How should Solomon judge the case. Bring me a sword! he says, and then he pretends to measure the baby into halves. And one woman is heart-broken. No! she cries. Give the baby to her! But the other woman has this smug look on her face: Go ahead! she says. Fair's fair! And you know what's happening?! Life isn't fair. One woman's baby died! And in the cruelty of her crushed spirit, envy leaps into her heart, and she says: If I can't have my baby, why should she have hers?! That's the difference between envy and covetousness, isn't it? Covetousness wants what someone else has. But envy wants only to take away from others what I can't have for myself. Shel Silverstein put it in a little prayer in one of his great children's books: Now I lay me down to sleep. I pray the Lord my soul to keep. If I should die before I wake, I pray the Lord my toys to break so the other kids can't play with them! If I can't have them, neither should they! If I can't have God's blessing, neither should Abel! So Cain went out and killed his brother. So one high school girl went out and killed the cheerleader. If you've ever been hurt in life, and who hasn't... If you've ever been passed over for a promotion, if you've ever been struck down by a disease or a disability you didn't count on, if you've ever watched others sail right on through waters that swamped your boat, or soar through winds that plastered your carcass all over the cliff, then you know this path. And you know as well the beast of envy that lurks on it.

Back in the fourth century, there was a great preacher in Caesarea, on the shores of the Mediterranean Sea. His name was Basil, and he once preached a sermon that he simply called: On Envy. And he said in that sermon that there were three ways in which envy twists us, once it's bitten our hearts. He said these were the symptoms we could look for, if we wanted to know the power of this disease in our lives.

For one thing, he said, envy turns us into hpocrites and liars. Not boldly so, maybe. But always, in some way, a little less than truthful.

Not so long ago it happened in a sick way in a small community in New Jersey, down in the States. A rural town, three churches struggling to survive. Then one of the churches called a pastor who was extremely gifted. His sermons were relevant and gripping. His personality had the loving compassion of Mother Teresa coupled with the dynamic charisma of Mel Gibson. He could teach in ways that made people hungry for more. People saw God in his ministry! Of course, you know what happened. Folks began to drift from the other two churches and find their way into his church on Sundays. And that's where the problems began. Because the other two pastors met together. And they decided that surely God was not in such a flamboyant style of ministry. Obviously he preached a false gospel. And then they started some rumors that maybe there might be some kind of sexual indiscretions going on. And the rumors spread. And the people wondered. And the pastor's family was shamed. And in a short while they left town. Envy found its mark. It turned two preachers of the truth into liars. And it made the cross of Jesus Christ a hypocrisy.

Envy and slander are close friends, aren't they? There's a French Proverb that says: It is only at the tree loaded with fruit that people throw stones. And Francis Bacon put it like this: He that cannot possibly mend his own case will do what he can to impair another's. That's one of the trademarks of envy in our lives.

Here's the second one that Basil noted. He said the envious are never truly thankful, because they never truly believe they have sufficient in life. Their eyes always rove the stock on other people's shelves. **An envious person doesn't know gratitude**.

Thorstein Veblen, a leading economic theorist, says that much of the consumerism in North America is fed by a marketing plan that roots itself in envy. Keep them drooling for bigger and better and more expensive products, he says. Never, never, never hint that enough is enough! Veblen calls it "conspicuous consumption." Get people to notice other people who have things they don't have, and the money markets will jingle!

51

Hello! Are you alive out there?! You know what he's talking about, don't you?!

The third test of envy in our souls, said Basil, was the test of negative focus. Somehow, he said, those who are envious of others seem to be the most negative people in society. People with a negative disposition tend to have the cancer of envy eating away inside. They focus only on the worst of life, and can't find the best.

Recently I read *The Autobiography of Malcolm X*. Powerful book! I hope the movie will be able to capture it! Malcolm X talks about his younger years. Blacks had nothing, Whites had everything. That's how he saw it. And he wasn't alone. You know what he did? He used to buy skin creams that promised to lighten his skin color! White is better, right?! Black is bad, bad, bad! He used to get his hair "conked." That's what they called it. They made a foul-smelling potion of lye and other chemicals and then they soaked their heads in it till their scalps burned raw. And then they took a hot iron of sorts, and they seared the curls out of their hair. Just to be like a white person. It was all part of life on the envy side of the street. Anything about his natural life was bad.

But, hey! I do it too. I play with enough false humility to wish myself someone else. Often! Sometimes all I see is the worst of me. And when I do that envy kicks in overtime. A negative outlook on life and envy are constant companions.

Our guide through the jungle: deepening faith, quickening love.

I walk through the jungles with Cain an awful lot. And envy dogs our heels. Sometimes it bites and poisons. And many times there's spilled blood on the path around me. The blood of Abel. The blood of rivals. The blood of friends.

But always, when we walk there, Cain and I, there's other blood too. And it's the cure for the poison of envy. It's the blood that was spilled in raging envy and righteous jealousy in the streets of Jerusalem 20 centuries ago. It's the blood that stained the earth, and fouled every beast lurking in the shadows. It's the blood of Calvary, the blood of the cross, the blood of Christ.

Let me tell you where envy haunts me most these days. It's in the team ministry that we share here at First Church, especially Pastor Peter and I. For four years now we've rubbed shoulders together. And it's been really good, but it hasn't always been easy. Sometimes I envy his gifts and his experience. Sometimes I envy the place he's gained in some of your hearts, a place I can't seem to find. Sometimes I envy the wisdom and insights and leadership skills he shows. And often Cain comes to visit with me in my study. He sits in the chair across my desk. And we chat together about Pastor Peter. I'm sure you know what we talk about. And during those moments, the beast reaches out from the shadows under my desk, and bites my heart. And I can see the delight in Cain's eyes. And we smile together. And we get ready to do a little bloodletting. And sometimes some of you help us along. Because you see our different personalities. And you feed our suspicions. And you taunt our jealousies. And the carpet grows crimson up there at 507 Talbot.

But then comes Tuesday morning. And here's where the beast gets tamed. Because Cain has to move off his chair. Pastor Peter comes in and he sits there. And we talk together. And we share our hearts. And we love each other. And we pray for each other. And the truth of scripture is this: You cannot envy a person you love! Remember how the Apostle Paul put it, I Corinthians 13? He said: Love is patient and kind; it does not envy...!

King Saul envied young David because Saul didn't love him. But Saul's son Jonathan didn't envy David one bit, because he loved David with a love surpassing that of women, says the Bible. A mother can't envy the achievements of a daughter she loves! A child can't envy the abilities of a friend she loves! A teen can't envy the talents of a brother he loves! And the beast is tamed by love.

Where is your brother? God asks Cain. But Cain doesn't know. You see, he doesn't have a brother. He didn't have a brother even when Abel was alive, because he never really loved Abel! That's why he could kill Abel. Read Shakespeare's *Othello*! You can't find a clearer, more powerful picture of envy than that. And you hear the ringing cry: O! beware, my lord, of jealousy. It is the green-eyed monster which doth mock the meat it feeds on. You know it, don't you?!

But you know this too. At least you should after being in this place this morning. You know that envy is tamed by love. Love is the only safe guide through the jungles of the beast. Love is the only leash that can hold it in check. And you know that love grows also on spilled blood. The blood of Christ. Don't ask me to explain it. Mysteries aren't always there to be explained. But don't try to fight the beast without it either. You'll lose. Every time. Because only those who know the caring compassion of Christ find the antidote that keeps envy at bay.

Wrestling
Homecoming
Genesis 32:1-3, 22-32; Matthew 26:36-46;
Ephesians 6:10-13

Get the picture! Jacob's coming home! Now, for most of us that's a rather nice thing to have happen. Homecoming weekend on the campus is a riot! And coming home from a hard day's work or a night at the hospital...it's one of the best things we can experience. Talk to travelers at Christmas time, and you'll find that 9 out of 10 are "going home," whatever that means for them. Well, Jacob's going home too. But, for him it's a lonely business. You see, he's been away from home these last 14 years: went over to Uncle Laban's place in the Old Country to learn farming for a while. It went okay for him, but it was sort of a mixed blessing. You've got to understand it... Jacob has one of those crazy lives: he succeeds at everything he does, but he's always in the doghouse for it. Maybe it's his name. You know what his name means, don't you?! Cheat! That's what his folks called him. Cheater and Swindler! That's what the name "Jacob" means! And it's true! Life for him is a game, a con-game. It's like the song says: he's always just one step ahead of the shoeshine; two steps away from the county line!

Jacob left home fourteen years ago because he cheated his brother. Papa Isaac was on his last legs: couldn't see much anymore, hearing was pretty poor, thought he better settle family matters before he died. So he called in his oldest son Esau to give him the keys to the estate. Only Jacob managed to get there first. He tricked his dad into thinking he was his brother. And then he had to run for his life when Esau found out!

Things weren't much better at Uncle Laban's place, though... Jacob tried to be nice at first. But then he found out that his uncle was a lot like him. Uncle Laban was a cheat, too! Jacob falls in love with cousin Rachel, but when he asks her dad if he can marry her, Laban makes him work as a slave for 7 years first! That's a good way to get cheap labor, isn't it?! I think I'll do that! Here's a warning, guys... If any of you wants to marry one of our daughters, you'll have to write sermons for me first for seven years. I like that! That's a pretty good deal! But listen to this: that's not the end of it for Jacob! They finally get to the wedding night, and Uncle Laban throws this huge party! Must have been a little drinking going on, because Jacob's not very with it by the time he goes to bed. He takes his bride into the honeymoon suite, and they spend the night together, and then, in the morning, he looks over at her, and surprise! Surprise! It's not Rachel there in bed with him! It's her older sister Leah instead! (Does this sound like a soap opera yet?!) Oh! says Uncle Laban, when Jacob comes storming in to work that morning, you see, we can't let Rachel marry until her older sister gets hitched! Otherwise people will think that she's no good!

So Uncle Laban tricks Jacob into working another 7 years for him, just to buy Rachel as his second wife. And then, just to get even, Jacob tricks Uncle Laban. He starts collecting all the runts from the herds, and he breeds them for himself, till he has more cattle than his uncle does! And they carry on like that for awhile, eyeing each other, suspicious and jealous. It's a nasty time in the Old Country. But finally comes a straw that breaks the camel's back. Rachel's learned a thing or two from her husband. Maybe even from her dad. In any case, she manages to cheat her father out of the family gods. Those were little statues that they kept in the house. Supposedly, if you found the right ones, they'd bring you good fortune. Now, Rachel stole them away one evening. That's a pretty mean thing to do. People in those days thought that all the best luck went along with the family gods. So when Laban loses the little gods he's plumb out of luck! And that's the end of this episode. Maybe we should call it "As the Stomach Churns"! In any case, the old Country's not big enough for the both of them anymore, so Uncle Laban puts a sword to Jacob's neck and he sends him packing.

So here's Jacob, a day's journey from home. And he's nervous! You can bet your bottom dollar he's nervous! This past Monday night a couple of our girls kept saying it: Oh, I'm so nervous! I'm so nervous! They'd been gone from school for just three months, and they were so nervous about going back. Would their friends remember them? Would their teachers be nice? Well, that's nothing compared to Jacob: 14 years he's been gone! You know he's on edge. What'll he find? I think, maybe, he was actually hoping that some people had forgotten him. Like Esau, you know! So he sends out some scouts. And this is the word they bring back. Well, they say, your brother Esau hasn't forgotten you! He's got 400 men, armed and mounted, and they're headed this way! Talk in the streets is that you'll be mincemeat by this time tomorrow!

So Jacob starts scheming again. First, he sends presents on ahead to Esau. Big presents, like most of his herds of cattle! He sends the gifts in several sections, just to make sure Esau gets the idea! Then he divides the rest of his large caravan into two groups. His mind is spinning: If Esau's still angry, he thinks, after he gets my presents he'll come charging in with his armed men! But maybe I can fool them. If we split this big company in two, maybe he'll come after the wrong group, and I'll be able to get away! And then comes Jacob's greatest strategy for self-preservation: he sends his wives and his children across the river in the dark of the night. Wasn't easy, but it makes things safer for him. He goes back and stays alone, all by himself on the other side! He knows that even if Esau does manage to get this far, when he attacks the camp across the river, Jacob should hear the screams of the women and kids, and that'll just give him enough time to sneak off into the deserts! See what a nice guy Jacob is?!

Jacob wrestles with himself.

And there he sits alone. We know what he's thinking, don't we?! You've been there too, and so have I. We sit alone. We've done all we can to protect ourselves. We won't know till tomorrow whether we'll get away with it, and there we sit, stewing in the darkness: anxious, fearful, wondering. This may be a soap opera, but isn't that the cleverness of soap operas. They don't portray the humdrum lives we lead everyday: we don't want them too! That's too boring! What they do is act out the nighttime fantasies of our souls: the mad romantic passions we hide so well; the dark schemes we'd never admit during the day, even the secret fears of fate and chance turning against us! We may not want Jacob for a neighbor. But we share his lonely retreat too often. There we are with him: knotted up and remorseful, anxious and alone.

This past week someone sat in my study: she knew where Jacob was at--sleepless through the night, tortured by the past, uncertain about the future.

Said F. Scott Fitzgerald, "At 3 o'clock in the morning, it's always the dark night of the soul." And so it is for Jacob. You know the restlessness: anxious and alone.

God wrestles with Jacob.

But here's the crazy thing: Jacob isn't alone! Something moves in the shadows! Someone challenges him from the night! Someone even comes close to him, grabs hold of him, pins him to the ground and wrestles him in deadly earnest. Who are you?! shouts Jacob. Who are you?! But the stranger is silent. He moves like a ghost, even if he grapples like a champion.

There's a scene in the book of Job that pictures it so well. It comes in chapter 4. Job sits in silence, broken, cruelly hurt. Then his friend Eliphaz comes to him and starts talking. He says, I know what you're going through, Job. He says, "...a word, in secret, came to me, a whisper crept in my ear, at night, when visions flash and ecstasy grips the mind. Terror caught me; panic shook my bones like sticks. Something breathed on my face; my hair stood stiff. I could barely see--a spirit-- hovering on my chest...." (4:12-15) So it came to Jacob that night. Was it just his conscience battling with him? The past coming back to haunt him, to drive him mad?

No. You've battled your conscience, and so have I. And too often we come away the winner. Jacob was a better lawyer for the defense than most of us. If his conscience had attacked him, he would have won in three rounds or less.

It has to be something more that wrestles with Jacob this night. It's something like the "Presence" that haunts us, dogging our footsteps, lurking just to the right of our field of vision, hiding in our shadows. You know what I mean. Francis Thompson called it the "Hound of Heaven," the one who pursued him down the corridors of the universe, with "noised feet" and "deliberate speed;" and "majestic instancy." And we run from him. And we stumble along blindly, not knowing where we're going, but knowing that we want to get away, we want to break free, we want to escape. But the faster we run, and the longer we hide, and the more desperate we struggle, the more persistent he becomes.

So God wrestles with us.

Who are you?! we cry with Jacob. Who are you, pursuing us so madly?! Fighting us so fiercely?! Taking hold of us so strongly?!

But we know, don't we?! We know, like Jacob knew. Francis Thompson called him Love. Constant Love. A Love that will not let us go, that races after us, that catches hold of us, that wrestles with us, till we see his face in the morning light.

A brilliant scientist, Loren Eiseley, tells of a troubled time in his life. He knew all the answers, in scientific terms. But still he didn't know the meaning of his life. He went to speak at a conference in a large city, took a cab from the airport. They drove through a dark side of that metropolitan world, slums and broken factories, crumbling houses, even an overgrown cemetery. It was a picture of his own gloomy thoughts. Suddenly, as the cab turned a corner, there was a sign. A piece of plywood with these words on it: **Christ died to save mankind. Is it nothing to you, all ye that pass by?** And Eiseley tells how the words dug in. Is it nothing to you? they asked him. Is it nothing to you? So often I had passed by, he said. So often I had run and run and run, never stopping to think what it was that I was running from. A picture of Christ, agonizing in the Garden, wrestling with the Father: Let's try another way! he says. Must we rescue them?! he prays. Save me and let them go! he pleads. But you know that's not what happened that night. The wrestling in the Garden. And the wrestling for your soul.

One of you came to London to go to school some years ago. You came running from your home community, running from your parents, running from things that were old and dead for you. You found something different here. You managed your escape. Or so you thought. But Love came looking for you. Love came searching for you, on "noise'd feet," with "deliberate speed," and "majestic instancy." And you ran, and you wrestled, and you fought to be free... And your Lover wouldn't let you go. And your Lover took hold of your soul. And you're a member of this church today, because God Himself wrestled you in with His grace.

Because we also wrestle with ourselves.

And why? Why does God wrestle with us? Why did God wrestle with Jacob that night? You know why, don't you? It's because Jacob needed to become something more than he was by himself: more than just a cheat, and a scoundrel, and a swindler. Jacob needed a new name. And that's what God gave to him, in the wrestling. People won't call you Jacob anymore, he said; You've got to have a new name! Here it is: ISRAEL! That's what they'll call you! ISRAEL! They'll call you that, because I call you that! And you know what it means, don't you?! It means: one who wrestles with God!

Think of it! We wrestle every day. We wrestle with our jobs: should we play the game or not? A friend of mine says he's so sick of it. You've got to play the game, he says, or you don't get the promotion. Who's palms are you going to grease this time? Who's back are you going to scratch? Who's behind are you going to...? A young woman recently quit a job here in London. Couldn't stand it anymore, she said. Every day I sold a little more of my soul! The wrestling! The wrestling! A man died last week. His widow said: He was bitter at the end! Forty years ago he came here from Holland. He had a dream! She said: I saw his work kill off every part of that dream. Why? What happened to him? The wrestling. It ground him down. It wore him out. He was only

61

a shell of the man I married, she said, when he died. And she shook her head in bitterness.

We wrestle with our relationships. Gordon McDonald, the great preacher, tells how he almost bargained away his marriage. Wonderful wife, two terrific kids,... but he let his ego grow with his fame, and pretty soon he began to believe the things they said about him. And when his wife didn't praise him enough, and when his kids took too much of his time, and when people demanded more than he could give, he went to someone else, a good friend, a fellow Christian. She seemed to understand him so much better. It was all so innocent at the time, so pious, so caring and godly... You know what he's talking about. The wrestling.

Some know it on the single's scene too... A local bartender says that he knows some of you quite well. He's a bit ashamed about it, when he talks with me. But that's the way it is. You know the wrestling. What's there to do at night? you ask yourself. You put your time in at work, and then you've got these next seven hours to kill. And you wrestle with your spirit. Who am I? What's my life all about? Where am I going? And you try to find a name of respect for yourself. But too many mornings you wake up with your money gone, and in the wrong bed.

You know the wrestling: the wrestling with pain and with pride, the wrestling with hopefulness and with hopelessness, the wrestling with strength of energy and weakness of spirit. You know the wrestling of your life.

And God will not let us go.

And here's the gospel for you this morning. God wrestles with you too! And God won't let you go! Jacob did all he could that night to free himself. He fought for his life! You know he did! But in the morning, here's the surprise: He found that it didn't really matter anymore.

62

Because God wasn't out to take his life away from him. God was only going to make sure he had a life to live when the wrestling was over.

Think of it this way. A publisher once asked a famous preacher to write a book. The publisher was very specific. He wanted the preacher to write a book about conversion. He even assigned the author a title for the book. He was supposed to call it: ***How Can I Find God?*** And so the preacher wrote a book to fit that title. But later he said to himself: Now, that's really silly, isn't it?! Can a fish "find" the ocean? Can a bird "find" the skies? Can a tree "find" the earth? Of course not! There is no fish without the ocean! The bird doesn't exist without the skies! The tree is formed from the earth, rooted in the earth, sustained by the earth! How can the fish find the ocean? Or the bird find the skies? Or the tree find the earth? And how can I find God? What a silly question! Isn't it God who finds me?! Who forms me?! Who frames my life in His love and care?!

And so God wrestles with us. For the self that runs from him, runs like a fish out of water, runs like a bird falling from the heavens, runs like a tree losing its roots. Think of the things we say: I don't really feel like myself today. I'm so ashamed of myself! I forgot myself there for a moment! I just hate myself! What are we saying? What's really happening to us? Remember what the father said to his daughter, the little girl he abused time and again, for years on end?! Remember what he said to her the first time they got back together. He was out of jail, on parole... He said: I'm so sorry for what I've done to you!!! I don't know what to say!!! I wish I weren't myself!!!

There's the wrestling of God with us. We think we make our way in life, we think we know the self that's best for us, we think we can find a way to swim outside of the ocean, a way to fly without looking up to the heavens or to grow without digging deep. But we can't, can we?! We can't, and we can't, and we can't, till Love wrestles us in the night, and gives us a new name. You are Israel, he says. You wrestle with God! And then we find ourselves again.

And when we're wrestled back to God, He shares the wrestlings of our lives.

The wrestling doesn't end, of course. You see Jacob walking down to the river the next morning. He's limping. He won't forget this night. He'll always be reminded of the struggles that tore him apart, and the wrestling that put him back together. The wrestling is never easy. And it marks him for all the days to come. Just like it marks you here today. God is wrestling with your spirit this morning. You can try what you will, but you can't escape. This is a place of wrestling, And here you see Him this morning, wrestling in the Garden over your soul, wrestling on the way to the cross for your life, wrestling with the powers of evil to bless you, and to give you a new name.

And all your life the wrestling continues. Elizabeth Achtemeier teaches preaching at Union Theological Seminary, in Richmond, Virginia. I once wanted to go to that school, and study with her there. She says that one of the greatest errors of young preachers is their desire to tell people that it's very easy to know the will of God. It's so easy to preach in Black and White, to declare This or That, with no shades of gray in between. But it's not so, she says. The wrestling continues: What jobs should we be looking for? Who should be our life partners? Where will we send our children to school? How do we care for the sinner while we condemn the sin? What's the right answer for Canada in the coming referendum? Do we walk out of the grocery store with paper bags that destroy trees, or with plastic bags that use up oil, or with cloth bags that pollute the waters when we wash them? How do we watch the starving children of Somalia on television, and then turn back to our rich and excessive meals, and throw the scraps in the garbage? The answers are rarely easy. They're rarely in Black and White. And our lives carry with them the struggles of choices made and often choices regretted. Would this Israel who faced Esau that day be different from the Jacob who shuddered in the shadows the night before? Not completely, you can be sure. He'd look within, and he'd see the self that's a cheater, and he'd see the self that's a saint; he'd see the self that wrestled with Laban, and he'd see the self that wrestled with God. And sometimes he'd choose the one and sometimes he'd choose the other. And we do too.

Paul says that we wrestle every day, against principalities and powers, against things within and things without, against spiritual forces and evil cheatings. Corrie Ten Boom tells the story in her book *The Hiding Place*... During the second World War, her family hid some of the Jews, to keep them from the gas chambers. She said that she and her father needed to find a safer place for one Jewish mother and her very young child. She says that a local clergyman came into their watch shop one day. They asked him if he would take these two frightened ones into his home. But the pastor refused. Corrie couldn't believe it. On an impulse, Corrie ran to the mother, and grabbed the little baby from her arms. She brought him to the pastor, and she tried to thrust him into the pastor's hands. But he refused. No! he said. Definitely not! We could lose our lives for that Jewish child! he said. And who could blame him? How could he help others, if he himself were dragged away to the concentration camps? That was the self he listened to when he made his choice.

You see, it's not always easy. Father Ten Boon collected the little one in his arms, and he said to the pastor: You say we could lose our lives for this child. I would consider that the greatest honor that could come to my family! Another self. Another choice. And you and I face it every day in the wrestling of our lives.

That's why this church is so important to you. Do you know what it's all about? This church is a community of wrestling. Here you find those who share your struggles of life. Here you find others who know what you face. Here you find women and men, girls and boys, who've spent dark and lonely hours on the hillside at the Jabbok River, and who take to the struggles with you. What do we do in worship, from week to week, but wrestle with God. And He with us.

For here, in the sacrament, we find again His promise: I will never leave you! I will never forsake you! And it's His wrestling that brings us home.

> "Where cross the crowded ways of life,
> Where sound the cries of race and clan,
> Above the noise of selfish strife,
> we hear your voice, O Son of Man.
> In haunts of wretchedness and need,
> On shadowed thresholds dark with fears,
> From paths where hide the lures of greed,
> We catch the vision of your tears."
> --Frank Mason North

Three Kinds of Morality
Luke 9:46-56; 10:25-37

Six-and-a-half years ago I didn't know much about London, [Ontario]. I'm not sure how much I know about it today, but I think I know more about it now than I knew about it then! After the Search Committee of this church first contacted me about the possibility of becoming pastor here, we tried to find out more about the city of London and its people. We were living out in Alberta at one time. And one Sunday morning, after we'd accepted the call to come here, we were in church with Brenda's parents: Granum, Alberta. And a fellow came up to me. He was quite excited. He knew we were moving to London soon. He had a clipping in his hand from the Lethbridge *Herald*. He wanted me to see it. The dateline was "London, Ontario." And the story was about the Deputy Mayor of London, a man named Jack Burghart. It seems he had been arrested by the police for erratic driving, and for refusing to take a breathalizer test! This fellow in Alberta said that he just wanted us to know what a den of sin we were getting ourselves into! I had my work cut out for me in London, he said. Even the Deputy Mayor there was a drunk!

Well, we know now that Jack Burghart is nothing of the sort, that he's a fine community leader, and that he's publicly known for his faith and his integrity. But questions of morality like that surround all of us, no matter who we are. Some time ago Newsweek magazine carried a little comment about that. It seems that the FBI were investigating an attempted murder. Someone had put cyanide into a businessman's water cooler. Turned out to be one of his employees. But, said FBI Agent Anthony Nelson, in all fairness, there were others who didn't get along with him (either). He's a very difficult man to work for! Do you see the moral judgments that he's making? So maybe murder's not so bad if all you're doing is trying to kill a nasty person?!

Or think of this: one of the big polling firms recently asked this question of folks like you and me: How much money would you have to have before you would have intercourse with a complete stranger?! (I don't know who comes up with these questions, but I was intrigued by the answers that were given.) Do you know that less than 2 percent of the people polled said that they wouldn't do such a thing at all, for any amount of money in the world?! Less than 2 percent. If you think that's surprising, listen to this! The answers for men and women were quite different. Women said, on the average, that it would take a bribe of at least $10,000 before they'd sell themselves like that. But men, on the other hand, said they'd need only $10. Period! That's all!

You may not like it, but that's the way it is. That's what people say. That's how they think. And the very fact that pollsters ask these kinds of questions means that for humans, Life is moral. It has some values attached to it, that stick with us, no matter what we believe. Life is moral. That's what separates us from the animals. To be human means to have the power to make value choices. Annie Dillard talks about that, in her marvelous book, *Pilgrim at Tinker Creek*... She says she went down to her little island one day, in the middle of the stream that ran past her home. She stopped in her tracks, she said. There was frog in the water, a species of frog that almost no one ever sees. And it was just sitting there! It didn't seem to be afraid of her! She was amazed at it! She stood there for awhile, very silently. She didn't want to scare it away. But then something really strange happened. The skin of the frog suddenly collapsed! Just like a balloon when somebody lets out the air! Poof! Right down into the water! She stepped closer. What in the world was going on?! And then she saw it--at the rear end of the frog there was a large water beetle. It had its jaws clamped over the frog's skin, and it was sucking the insides out of the frog! It was draining the frog empty! Just like that! Like a child sucking on a freezie on a hot summer's day! And all that was left was the skin.

And Annie said it shocked her. She said she couldn't believe what was happening. She said she wondered what kind of world this was, where creatures could do that kind of thing. But then, she said, she thought about how different those beetles and those frogs were from her as a human. The very reason that she was shocked by their behavior was because she was a human being. She could give that action a moral judgement. In fact, she couldn't help but make moral judgments about it. That was the difference between her and them. That's what made her human.

Humans are moral creatures. You can't suck the life out of another person and get away with it. Even if the law never catches you, your own soul catches you! You can't live without some code of ethics, some standards for behavior, some system of morality. You need those things to give structure to your world; even to give personality to your character. Maybe you've seen the "Hour of Power" on television?! Robert Schuller is the minister, and he broadcasts from the Crystal Cathedral, in Garden Grove, California. If you've ever seen the Crystal Cathedral, you know that it's all made out of glass! Solid glass on the outside! A huge church, just one pane of glass after another. Of course, to hold all of that glass in place, there's a skeleton of steel on the inside. And one day a woman went into the Crystal Cathedral to see it, and someone asked her what she thought of it, and she looked around, and she said, Well, it's going to be a real nice place, once they get this scaffolding out of here! But they can't do it, of course! Take away the steel skeleton, and the glass falls, and the cathedral collapses.

And so it is with us. Take away the moral fiber of a person, and you take away the very essence of who he is. That's why it was so important for this man to talk to Jesus, in Luke 10. He knew that he was a moral creature. He knew that his whole life was bound up in his social ethics. But society was changing, and he wanted to hang onto his values. And that's why, when he comes to Jesus, he's serious! It's more than just a question of theology that he has. It's more than just a creedal statement that he's looking for. He's digging to the root of his character: What must I do to inherit eternal life?! he asks. What code of ethics will help me survive, will bring me closer to God?!

Well, says Jesus, do you know what the scriptures say? Sure, he says. And then he recites some words about loving God and about loving other people. Great, says Jesus. You're on the right track!

But here comes the crunch. What does it mean to love other people? Who are we supposed to love? And how are we supposed to love them? You see, morality is defined in different ways by different people. Remember Wilhelm Goering?! He was the man who founded the Gestapo, the Nazi secret police. Do you know what he had on the wall of his office? His office, where he plotted the extermination of the Jews? His office that breathed with the horrors of torture, that created the specter of the concentration camps, the death camps, the mass graves, the gas ovens? This is what Wilhelm Goering had on his office wall. He had a sign that said: "He who tortures animals wounds the feelings of the German people!" Can you see it?! Can you imagine it?! Kill the Jews, but don't hurt the animals. And Wilhelm Goering considered himself a very moral person.

Which morality shall I follow? asked this man in Luke 10. And to answer him, Jesus tells a little story. A little story about the different kinds of morality. Three different kinds of morality.

Social Morality

A man was walking down the road from Jerusalem to Jericho, says Jesus. It goes downhill all the way--it starts at a kilometer above sea level in Jerusalem, and by the time you get to Jericho, at the northern end of the Dead Sea, you're half-a-kilometer below sea level. That's why Jesus says he was walking down the road. Now, it happened to be a very bad stretch of road, worse, even, than the 401! There were caves all over in the sides of the hills, and robber bands made their homes there. When General

Pompey held the reigns of power in Palestine, he had to send an entire squadron of soldiers down there to deal with the bands of robbers and henchmen. The Crusaders later built a fort half-way down the road. It was the only way they could offer some safety to pilgrims walking that road. Well, says Jesus, this fellow was all by himself. And when the robbers came out of the hillsides, he was easy pickings. They stole his goods, and they stripped him of his clothes, and they beat him, and then they left him for dead.

Now, notice that Jesus doesn't tell us where this man was from. Was he a Jew? We don't really know. In fact, there were at least 25 different distinct communities in the area. And they were all populated by peoples of diverse ethnic origins. Of course, being from the Middle East, they all had many of the same physical features--skin color, dark hair; things like that... But how could you tell them apart? How would you know that you were talking to a Jew, rather than a Nabitean? In two ways: one was by looking at the kinds of clothing he wore; and the other was by listening to the accent in his voice. Clothes and voice! Those were the ways you identified each other along the road.

But now, think of it again! The robbers did two things to this man--they took his clothes, and they left him half-dead. Now nobody can tell where he's from. They've taken away his identity. His clothes are gone, the distinctive clothes of his ethnic community. And they've beaten him so badly that he can't speak. He's nothing more than a generic man. No-name brand. In the truest sense of the term, he's a displaced person! He belongs to no community.

But here comes help for him, right?! Here comes a Jewish Priest down the road. Now, you've got to understand a few things about this Priest. In Jesus' day, the Priests were the upper class of society. They were the rulers of the people, under the Roman administration. And they had a lot of wealth and privilege. And you can be sure that no priest would be walking down this road all by himself.

71

He would either be in a company of other priests, where they could keep one another safe, or he'd be riding on a horse. And, this fellow is alone, says Jesus. So, he must be on horseback. Now, think of it!! If he was on foot, he wouldn't be able to help the man lying there very much. He wouldn't have any extra provisions. He couldn't lift the man and carry him out of there. All he could do would be sit with him and wait for someone else to come along with a horse so they could take him to a place of care. But this priest is alone. So he's riding a horse. He could very well take the man to safety and give him to others who might help him.

But what does he do? He passes right on by! says Jesus. Why? Not because he's an immoral person!! No sir! Don't even think that way for a minute! In fact, he passes by the man precisely because he's a very moral person. But his morality is a social morality. It has to do with the structures of his society. You see, he's probably going home to his family in Jericho. He's just spent two busy weeks leading worship services at the Temple in Jerusalem. And he's carrying his pay with him. How did they pay the priests in Jesus' day? They gave them part of the tithe that came in: meat from the sacrificed animals, grain from the fields, money from the love offerings. Now he's on his way to his family in Jericho, and they're all waiting for him there.

But there was one thing that could stop him from getting there. The written laws of the land said that there were five ways in which a Jewish person could become ritually unclean. Guess what topped the list? Touching a dead body! Think of it! The man doesn't move. He looks dead. If the priest comes within 2 meters of a dead body, he'll become ritually unclean. That's why you see him skirting the other edge of the road. Jesus says that he passed by on the other side. And another thing. The oral traditions of his society, passed down from generation to generation, said that there were four other things that could make him unclean. You know what was always named first? Contact with a non-Jewish person! So here he is. Even if that body over there isn't dead, he can't tell if the man is a Jew or not! No clothes. No voice. Now, what would happen if the priest would get too close to a dead body? Or what would happen if he touched a man who wasn't a Jew? Well, if he became ritually unclean, two things would happen to him. First, he'd have to throw away his pay from the Temple. He'd have to throw away the meat he was bringing home, and the grain, and the loaves of bread. If he became ritually impure, they'd become ritually impure as well! He couldn't use them anymore, and he couldn't bring them home to his family either. Secondly, then he'd have to turn right around and head back up to the Temple in Jerusalem for a whole week of purification rituals! No homecoming this week! Can you imagine it?! And if that's not bad enough, the purification rituals he'd have to go through, there at the temple, would require him to stand naked one day, in public, and have the gathering worshippers spit on him! Can you see it?! Last week he led the crowds in praise! This week he stands there scorned! That's what would happen to him if he touched a dead body, if he came into contact with a non-Jewish person.

But that's the morality of his society. And that's the social morality he buys into. A social morality that judges human behavior on the basis of one criteria: What will other people think?! What will other people think! Social morality is the strongest ethical power in any community. Why do you wear the clothes you do? Because most people in our society wear these kinds of clothes. Why do you schedule your day in certain ways? Because that's the way most people use their time in our society. Even in the church, social morality is the strongest ethical power.

Harry Emerson Fosdick once preached a sermon on ethics and morality. He called it "Six Ways to Tell Right from Wrong." And usually I really like the way he preached. But this sermon was something else. How can you tell right from wrong? he asked. In these six ways: if it has some common sense about it; if it makes for good sportsmanship; if it brings out the best in you; if it stands up to public scrutiny; if it's something your heroes would do; and if you can see that it would last into the future. Now, those may be good reasons for doing many things. But they're all social reasons. Social morality. Christianity has nothing to do with them. They're good things to do to keep you out of trouble. That's social morality.

But the problem with social morality is that it has no standards outside of itself by which to judge itself. You do things, like that priest did things, because that's what society says you should do. But there are two problems with that. For one thing, societies keep changing. So their standards for morality keep changing. Two hundred years ago, a Boston ship captain was arrested and forced to sit in stocks, bound hand and foot, for two hours in the Boston commons because of his "lewd and unseemly behavior." What did he do that was so wrong? What was his crime? Well, he just came back to Boston from a three-year voyage, and when he met his wife he kissed her. In public! Times change! And so does social morality. You see it all around you. Sometimes it scares you. Sometimes you don't know what to do about it. But that's the way it is when you try to live by it.

The second problem with social morality is that different cultures have different standards of morality. A few years ago, a member of our congregation told me how upset he was by a notice in our bulletin. He and his family have long since moved away. But that day he was quite perturbed. The notice in the bulletin said that the young people were going to get together on Sunday afternoon at a certain place in order to play softball. He didn't think that was right. He'd always been taught that you shouldn't play sports on Sunday. He knew times were changing. But he still didn't like it. So he took his teenaged children home, and they stopped at a McDonald's on the way for some food, and then he thought about it all afternoon long, while he went swimming in his pool. Swimming was okay on Sunday, but not a friendly game of softball. Eating out at a restaurant was okay on Sunday, but not the game in the park. Tyman Hoffman, retired minister in the Christian Reformed Church, tells how it was for him when he was a young lad in Holland. He went out for a date on a Saturday night. He stayed out later than he should have. He was biking home when he heard the bell in the clock tower strike midnight. He knew that he wasn't supposed to ride his bike on Sunday so he stopped, jumped off, threw the bike over his shoulder, and walked the rest of the way home.

Those things may make us smile, but there are others that can make us cry. Why could the Nazis exterminate the Jews during World War II? Because their society said it was wrong to hurt animals, but it was right to kill Jews. That's a social morality gone wrong. But it's still a social morality. And it thinks about life the same way this priest did in the story that Jesus tells. Social morality is strong. It can be decent and good. Or it can be evil and consuming. You know the power of evil. You know it in society. Remember the way that George Orwell put it in his classic novel, *1984*? Winston and O'Brien? Winston loves Julia. That's the one beautiful thing in his life, living in this dull, drab, dreary world of Oceania. O'Brien tortures Winston, gets him to confess all kinds of crimes. That's the way it is in the society of Big Brother. But in this one thing Winston shines. He will not betray Julia. He will not disown her love. All his morality is wrapped up in that one commitment. They can make him say anything else that they want. They can make him confess to all kinds of crimes, real or imagined. But this is his heart! This is his soul! This is his identity! He will never betray Julia! Nothing O'Brien can do will ever get him to break faith with her. Oh, says O'Brien, but there's always Room 101! And when they take Winston to Room 101, and when they strap his face into a hole in the side of a cage, and when they turn the hungry rats loose to eat his face, he cries, and he shouts: Do it to Julia! Do it to Julia! Just let me go! Do it to Julia! And Orwell says to us that anyone can be made to do anything. Morality is only the will of the one with the most power. That's the social morality of the Priest who walks by.

Rational Morality

There's a second kind of morality here, and that's the morality of the Levite. It's the morality of reason. The Levite sees the man at the side of the road too. Now, several things: First, he knew the priest was up ahead of him. He knew it because they left the Temple together. He knew it, too, because he saw the hoofprints of the priest's horse on the road. They were the last prints made. And he knew it because every traveler would ask as he left a village who was ahead of him. So he knows the priest came here before him. And he knows that the priest passed by without helping the man. Here's another thing; the Levite is bound by the same social codes as is the priest. He, too, mustn't make contact with a non-Jewish person, or he will become unclean.

But Jesus says that this man is ruled by a different morality than the social morality of the priest. The Levite actually goes over to the fellow on the ground and looks at him. Do you think he'll give him assistance? No, says Jesus. He moves on too. He's not under the spell of social morality, or he never would have gotten so close to the man. But his morality is one based on reason. His reasoning power is his guide. And this is probably what he's thinking: there's very little he can do for this man--he's near death; the Levite can't carry him to safety; he has no provisions to share with him there; and besides, the robbers who did this to him, might still be lurking nearby. He'd best get out of there as quickly as possible.

Rational Morality is better than Social Morality. It makes its choices, not just out of habit, or custom, or social pressure. It makes its choices by weighing the odds, and then deciding on the course of action which seems least harmful or most beneficial. Shakespeare dramatized it in *Romeo and Juliet*. We like to think of *Romeo and Juliet* as a love story. But it's so much more than that. It's a morality play. It's a morality play in which Rational Morality wins over Social Morality. The story is all about a feud, a bitter and deadly feud, between the families of the Montagues and the Capulets. Each family is very moral, in itself: courtesy, chivalry, caring... You find them in both houses. But still they kill one another in spite and in pain and in vengeance. That's the Social Morality they follow. "Be nice to your own people, but stick it to those of the other house." You know the old saying: All's fair in love and war! That's the Social Morality they live by. And that's the Social Morality they die by. Mercutio falls with the sword in his belly, and he shouts: A plague on both your houses! But when the young lovers, Romeo of the Montagues and Juliet of the Capulets, kill themselves, rather than bow to the unreasonable demands of that Social Morality, the shock of that horror wakes the reasoning powers of the fathers. And in the final scene, in his final words, Capulet stretches out his hand, and he cries: O brother Montague, give me thy hand!

And we applaud his Rational Morality. We know that it's better than Social Morality. Rational Morality is the morality of novels and of films and of poetic justice. It's the morality of Star Trek, and Star Trek: The Next Generation, and of science fiction stories of a time in the future, when humans will come to their senses, and will use their rational faculties to end all wars, to educate all criminals, and to find a way to put reason over passion and logic over emotion.

But Jesus says that the Levite still walks away from the man on the road. Even his Rational Morality will leave the man to die. And this won't be the only time that happens. Because Rational Morality is limited, as well. It may be better, generally, than the morality of society. But it has its own grave limitations.

For one thing, even our reason is tainted by evil. Sanctity and sanctimoniousness are close buddies. And our reasoning can't tell them apart. When are we doing the "right" thing, and when are we doing the self-serving thing? Our reasoning doesn't always know.

Willie Nelson, the country music singer, once bought his own golf course. Someone asked him what par was. And Willie said, "Anything I want it to be!"

That's logical, isn't it? He owns the course; he makes the rules. He said to the fellow, "See that hole over there? That's a par-47, and yesterday I birdied it!"

That's cute. But evil isn't. And in our minds it can act much the same way. The greatest criminals in human history weren't mentally incompetent. They weren't mentally deficient. Many were even geniuses. They managed to rig the game of life, in their minds, so that they could justify their crimes and always come out on top. It's the evil within us. It's bred in the bones. And it's sheltered in our minds as well.

The other reason why Rational Morality is limited is this: Which of our selves is our rational self? Can you tell?

There's a character in one of H. G. Wells' novels who says, "I'm not a man but a mob!" And so it is often with us. Today I'm this person, and I think this way; tomorrow there's another self in me that will come out and play.

To your own self be true? That's what Shakespeare says in *Hamlet* :

"This above all: to thine own self be true,
   And it must follow, as the night the day,
   Thou canst not then be false to any man."

But do we know our true self? Do we know which is the best? Can we find morality within? Will our conscience be our guide, or our reason, or our common sense? The Levite let his Rational Morality guide him. And he left the man to die.

The Morality of Love

And that's where we need to find a deeper morality for our lives, says Jesus, a higher morality. It's a morality that does not depend alone on the external peer pressures of society, like Social Morality does; and it's a morality that has more consistency than the internal leading of Rational Morality does. It's the morality of love.

The crowd around Jesus likes this story. They're getting into it now. They don't always care for their priests--"Holier than thou!" and all that. So when the Priest walks by they're not shocked at all. And it's the same with the Levite. Other religious figures might be good, but even they have their limitations.

So now they're waiting for Jesus to move on to the best part of the story. You see, they're sure he's going to talk about one of them. He'll say: "You know who came by next?! Just an ordinary fellow, a common, decent man on the street--sort of like you, or you, or you...." They crowd around Jesus. They want him to compliment them. They want him to tell them how good they are. They're sort of like the disciples of Jesus, who gathered around him a little while before. "Tell me I'm good!" they say. "Tell me I'm the greatest!"

And that's where Jesus shocks them out of their minds. Because he says it was a <u>Samaritan</u> who came next! A Samaritan! Come on, Jesus! Samaritans are immoral! Hey, just a little while ago James and John wanted to call down fire from heaven on them for being so mean and nasty. That's the way Samaritans are!

But that's the whole point of Jesus' story. He wants to shock the whatever out of them. Hey, that's why Ugo Cerletti first developed shock treatment. You know, where they hook wires up to your brain. Why? Because you can't break free from other patterns of thought or behavior. And the shock blows your mind. Literally! Till all the structures you knew are gone. And then you can start over.

I'll never forget how it was for a friend of mine in St. Louis, Missouri. She couldn't handle life anymore. She was bound up in depression and in a tight ball of destructive behavior. But they took her to a hospital. And they blew her mind with the shock treatment. When she came out later, she had found a new way to live.

So it is with Jesus' story here. He blows the minds of the crowds when he talks about a dirty Samaritan, and the Morality of Love. The morality of love never makes sense. And you'll never start thinking in its terms till you blow those other ideas of Social Morality and Rational Morality right out of your mind.

Do you know why you do the things you do? Do you know what lies beneath the surface of your morality? Is it the values of society? Even the society of the church? Probably so, for most of us. But then our morality is only a thin veneer. It's only a wallpaper we put up over our faces to look like the rest of the room we live in. Is your conscience your moral guide? God help those who don't meet up to our standards of decency! Said Aslan, the noble lion, to the children in Narnia, "There's a magic that goes back to before the beginning of time." Then he strapped his body to the stone cross. And he died to free young Edmund from a sickness he couldn't even name.

And there's the picture of the Samaritan on the road. The one who stops by your soul and lifts you up and wraps your fragile spirit in his cloak. And only those who've been to the inn of the Good Samaritan and who've rested under the coin of his care can find their way back to the road of life, the one that goes down from Jerusalem to Jericho, and follow his footsteps on that road. His morality is a magic that's deeper than Social Conformity. His morality is a power that's stronger than Rational Judgement. His morality is the morality of love. You can't always explain it. Just like you can't analyze a mother's caring for her child. But those who've themselves been lifted by love understand it.

Do you know it? Can you find it? Will you live by it?

"O Master, let me walk with thee
In lowly paths of service free!
Tell me thy secret, help me share
The strain of toil, the fret of care.

Help me the slow of heart to move
By some clear winning word of love:
Teach me the wayward feet to stay,
And guide them in the homeward way."

Finding Our Right Selves
Luke 18:9-17

Do you know why camels have humps? You do if you've read Rudyard Kipling's *Just So Stories*. He's got a tale there called "How the Camel Got Its Hump." It goes like this: When God first created the earth and all the animals, He gave each of the animals a different job to do. And all of the animals did their work. Except for one. Only the camel didn't do anything. Whenever the others animals asked the camel to help them, the camel just said, "Humph!!!" and he walked away. You see, the camel thought that he was so much better than all the other animals. He had too much pride. So whenever the other animals talked to the camel, he just said "Humph!!! and he walked away. And when God saw what was happening on earth, when He saw the silly pride of the camel, He collected all of the camel's "Humphs!!!" And he dumped them right onto the camel's back! And that's how the camel got its hump!

Proud people are kind of like camels, aren't they?! They stand out in a crowd. You can almost see their humps, humping up above everyone else! Do you know what they used to say about Mussolini? He was the proud little dictator of Italy 50 years ago. They said he could strut (even when he was) sitting down! Here's another one. Listen to this! "He was a solemn procession of one!" Can you see him, marching alone, in procession with himself! There's a proud man for you! See him humping above the crowds?!

Aren't you glad that you're not proud?! I'm so glad I'm not proud! You know, about the only thing I'm proud of is my humility. I'm sure proud of my humility!

Pride is a funny thing, isn't it?! We all have it, and we all hate it. In fact, one of Benjamin Franklin's most quoted quotes is this one. He said: The proud hate pride--in others! You know he's right.

That's why we love this little story of Jesus. He hits the nail on the head! Look! He's just been talking about how tough things can get in life, how rough it is for the small people, the needy, the widows and the orphans, the ones who cry out for justice, but nobody helps them. And all around him are people who know what he means. The hurting ones. The social outcasts. Who do you think we might find there in the crowd around him? A young man with AIDS? A bitter widow? A child with leukemia? A man who lives in a cardboard box in an alley off the street, who wears all of his clothes every day, and prays that the frost won't come tonight?

This is a good story for them! Two men went up to the temple to pray, says Jesus. One man stood up and said: God! I'm so thankful to be your faithful servant! I'm so thankful I'm better than anyone else! I'm so thankful I can do so many things for you! I just wish other people were like me!

The Separated Self

Now, what do you think?! You don't like him, do you?! You're not supposed to! He looks like a camel, humping around with his pride. And he sounds an awful lot like Narcissus. Do you remember Narcissus? The ancient Greeks and Romans used to talk about him. He was the fellow who never loved anyone around him, because he was always too much in love with himself. One day he was scrambling through the rocks of the hills on a hunt. And he got thirsty. And he found a little pool tucked away in the hollows. And as he bent down to take a drink, he found himself staring at his reflection in the water. He thought, at first, that it was a water nymph, come up to greet him. And he was so enamored by the beautiful face, by the wonderful eyes and the marvelous nose and chin, that he reached down into the water to embrace the nymph. But, of course, when he disturbed the surface of the water, the reflection seemed to scurry away. So he pulled back his hands, and he called out to the beautiful water nymph, and he cried tears of regret, and then, in a little while, he came back to him. And over and over this scene was repeated, Narcissus in love with himself, till he finally fell famished to his death!

But remember this! There were many who wanted to love Narcissus in his day! Many women tried to win his affections. They thought he was the greatest thing that had happened on earth! And so, too, there are many who want to love this man who prays in the temple that day! Pharisees were the good guys in Jesus' time. They wore white hats! We tend to write them off too quickly as hypocrites and frauds. But that's really unfair. The Pharisees were the moral fibre of the nation of Israel. If you want to make any comparisons to our day, then you'd have to see them running James Dobson's organization: Focus on the Family. That's the kind of people they were! All the best of morality and spiritual-ity was found among the Pharisees. The Sadducees had control of the powers of government in the land, but it was the Pharisees who held the respect of the people. Look! This Pharisee mentions tithing in his prayer. He says that he gives one-tenth of all his income to God through the ministries of the temple. Don't think that he's boasting about giving a lot of money! He probably didn't have half the wealth of the tax collector! Pharisees were notoriously poor! They came from the poorest corners of society. So he's not boasting about the great sums of money that he gives. He only tells God that he does what he can, even if it's not easy for him. How many of you, with as many bills as you have to pay, and with as small an income as you earn, have even begun thinking about

84

giving a tenth to God through the ministries of this church?! Don't jump to conclusions about how bad this fellow was! In fact, he says that he gives back to God a tenth of <u>all</u> he gets. Now, the tithe that was expected of the people was a tenth of whatever they earned as income. But the Pharisees broadened the practice. They even gave a tenth of their purchases in the market. If they bought ten onions, they'd give one to the poor. If they purchased a pound of flour, one tenth of it would go to feed the priests in the service of God. If they brought home five little quail to eat, half of one of them would be set aside, and then brought to the temple and burned as a sacrifice to God. They didn't have to do that. Everything that was sold in the marketplace had already gone through the tithing ritual. But the Pharisees wanted to make sure, they wanted to do things right, so they brought their tithes of it all anyway.

Another thing. Do you know why the Pharisees were called "Pharisees"? All of the Jewish writers of the first century tell the same story. The Pharisees got their name from the word that means "separate," or "holy." And the story behind that is this: there were laws for ritual cleansings at the temple, laws that told how the priests and Levites were supposed to wash their hands, and how they were supposed to handle the sacrifices brought to the altar. The Pharisees tried hard to live lives of holiness. So, they thought that if the temple laws were fitting expressions of worship there, one might think about using those laws to express holiness in daily living as well. And that's what happened. They took the holiness laws from the temple and they practiced them in their homes, and in their social interaction throughout the week. You could often recognize a Pharisee by the way in which he separated himself from others at mealtime, in order to practice certain rituals of cleansing. In fact, this Pharisee says that he fasts twice a week. Most people only fasted once a week. That's all the law required, in order to show sorrow for sins. But this man's a Pharisee. And the minimum requirements aren't enough for him. He doubles his acts of religious devotion.

Not only that. The Pharisees also tended to be on the leading edge of social reform. Do you know that 15 years before Jesus was born Herod the Great decided to test his popularity? He issued a decree that stipulated that everyone in the country had to stand before him, in rotation, and take an oath of unconditional loyalty to him personally. Josephus tells us what happened in his *Antiquities of the Jews*. He says that most of the people in Palestine took the oath. They were afraid of what might happen to them if they didn't. But there was one group that refused. The Pharisees. They announced that they couldn't take an oath to anyone but God. How many Pharisees were there? Josephus says that there were over 6000! And Herod punished every last one of them for defying him! Fifteen years later, in the year when Jesus was born, Herod's health was failing rapidly. It looked like he was going to die within hours. Two of the Pharisees, Judas and Matthias, seized the moment! They knew there would be quite some political turmoil after Herod died, so they gathered a group of younger men around them, and they climbed the wall at the main gate of the temple, and they tore down the huge golden eagle that Herod had put up there as a symbol of Roman authority. It was like the Russians toppling the statues of Lenin in Moscow a year ago. Only Herod wasn't dead. In fact, he recovered enough to make another public appearance. In Jericho. At the trial of Judas and Matthias. And he ordered them burned alive. And their co-conspirators.

All Pharisees!

Now, get back to Jesus' story. This man who comes to pray is a Pharisee. He's a godly man. He's a moral leader in the community. He's true to his God and he's true to his faith. You've got to admire him.

And there's the rub. Because he knows you've got to admire him! That's the point! He deserves it!

Tony Campolo tells about his seminary days. He had to take a course in homiletics under a Professor Albert Williams. Homiletics is the part of the seminary curriculum where they try to teach you how to preach. It's kind of a no-win job. If people learn how to preach, it's because they're good preachers. And if people don't learn how to preach, it's all your fault! Well, Professor Williams conducted his class like most homiletics professors do. He required each student to prepare and deliver a single sermon. And he and the rest of the class would sit in the benches of the chapel and evaluate that sermon. So here comes Tony. Everybody knows Tony Campolo today. He's one of the most sought-after speakers in North America. He's a very gifted preacher. And he was already then, even in his seminary days. So he served it up right. He says his sermon was perfectly prepared: a good outline, lots of illustrations, even a few jokes, just to keep them awake. And when he got to the conclusion, he knew that he'd preached to their hearts. He could feel it! That sermon was powerful! He says: In short, I knew I was good! And so did his classmates! Boy, did they ever like his sermon! They heaped on the praise! He'd go places as a preacher! they said. He was one of a kind! He certainly had a gift from God! Tony was beaming! Life doesn't get much better than this! And he couldn't wait for Professor Williams' evaluation. That would just make his day! So he flipped through all the papers. Dr. Williams' evaluation was the bottom one on the pile. He pulled it out. He held it up. He read it quickly. Just a single line. It didn't mention the content of his message. It didn't praise him for his delivery. It just said this: "Tony, you can't convince people that you're wonderful and that Jesus is wonderful in the same sermon."

You can't convince people that you're wonderful and that Jesus is wonderful in the same sermon! Do you see what he's saying?! Listen again to the Pharisee's prayer: God, I thank you that I am not like other men-- robbers, evildoers, adulterers--or even this tax collector. I fast twice a week and give a tenth of all I get. I can see Professor Williams sitting there in the Temple, next to Jesus. He's scribbling something on a piece of paper. He hands it to the Pharisee. The man holds it up and he reads it. Not much. Just a single line. It says: You can't convince God that you're wonderful and that He's wonderful in the same prayer.

What was the thing Jesus didn't appreciate about the Pharisee? It was that he used his prayer to try to convince God and to convince the others around him that he was wonderful. And he did it by separating himself from them. Notice what Jesus says: The Pharisee stood up and prayed... What? About himself?! Yes, he did that. But more. The way it says it in Greek is this: He stood up and prayed by himself... Alone! With no one else around him! The word is auto: you know, like automobile--a car that doesn't need horses because it can pull itself around; or autobiography--the story of your life that you write yourself; or an automatic pilot that flies the airplane without the pilot's help. This man prays auto--alone; by himself; separated from the others in the Temple.

Remember that most people came to the temple at the same time. Sure, there'd always be a few lingering around during the day, maybe widows and retired folk. But the rest of the people in Jerusalem would all go up to the Temple together: twice a day--once for the mid-morning sacrifice, around 9 a.m., and again for the mid-afternoon sacrifice, at about 3 p.m. Everybody would go--hundreds of folks are there. Mostly the same people, day after day. And you get to know each other. You know how it is here: most of you are sitting in the same benches that you sat in last Sunday, and the Sunday before. It's force of habit! You get to know the other people around you. And so it is with this fellow. He knows others around him. He sees others around him. He even mentions this tax collector in his prayer. He's aware of who the guy is, and what he does.

But he prays alone, by himself, separated from the others. That's the self he owns. That's the person he is. And that's the extension of his pride. He stands alone.

Last year, *Newsweek* magazine carried some interesting reflections on the late great war in the Persian Gulf. Saddam Hussein, said one article, was a very proud man. He needed to prove that he could stand alone. He needed to earn his respect in the world, even if it meant a million deaths in his own country. He's a proud man, said *Newsweek* (February 25, 1991, pp. 34-35). But, get this. In the same issue of *Newsweek* there was another article, this one an analysis column by George Will. And Mr. Will said that one of the reasons the U.S. pushed for battle with Saddam Hussein, was in order to win back its national pride! Vietnam hurt us, say some, because we didn't win that war. Let's have a fight we can win. Then we'll be proud again! And pride bends sword against sword, and weapon against weapon, till we've proved which corpse is better than the other.

It's a horrible thing out there--this demon of pride. But it's even more horrible in here! In my heart! Inside myself. And of all the prides in the world, none is so devious, so dastardly, so demonic, as religious pride.

How does the Friesian story put it?! The one about Fouke the baker in the town of Faken? He's a righteous man alright. So righteous that no one can match his constant display of piety. In fact, when he catches his wife Hilda in the arms of another man, everyone knows that he'll call down the curses of heaven on her and send her away in her disgrace. After all, she's violated the most sacred trust of human society. But here Fouke surprises everyone. He forgives Hilda! He actually forgives Hilda! And he keeps her there with him in his home! And then, he spends every waking hour despising her! That's the lure of pride. That's the temptation of righteousness. That's the separation that concerns Jesus. When your godliness sets you apart, watch out! Your ugliest self is showing.

Frederick Buechner puts it this way. He says: "...pride is a sin when, instead of leading you to share with others the self you love, it leads you (rather) to keep your self in perpetual safe-deposit. You not only don't secure any interest that way," he says, "but (you) become less and less interesting every day."

The separated self. The self that tells ethnic jokes about people from other groups. The self that defines success in terms of achievement. The self that identifies Christianity by way of denominational superiority. They're all the same. They pray auto, alone, by themselves, in the temple built for pride. That's the separated self.

The Swallowed Self

There's another self in this story. You see him groveling there on the floor. The tax collector. He's a traitor, you know. A traitor to his own countrymen. How did the Romans manage to keep their troops supplied while stationed in Palestine? They did it by taxes. They taxed the local citizens to pay for their own bondage. But they didn't send around tax forms in the mail. And they didn't collect T-4 slips. Instead, they sold tax franchises to the highest bidder. The person who promised to bring in the most money got the job of tax collector. He could collect as much as he wanted, so long as he brought to the Roman officials the amount that they had bargained for. So tax collectors were traitors and thieves. They worked for the enemy. And they padded their pockets with the excess they managed to skim from their neighbors' goods.

But something's happened to this man. We don't know what. All we know is that he's not very proud. In fact, he's swallowed his pride, and most of his self along with it. Men don't usually beat on their chests. It's not a "manly" thing to do. Actually, about the only time it happened was at a funeral when grief took over, and no one cared about appearances.

Maybe that's why it's appropriate here. The man's self has died. He's swallowed it. And all that's left of him is this sobbing, slobbering, sulking hulk, wondering where to go from here. He's like a black hole, really. You know, in outer space... A dark depression of dense matter that wraps itself around itself in heaviness. And nothing can unwrap it. It just grows deeper and darker and more dour by the moment.

That's the man here. That's the swallowed self.

See-Through Self

91

But there's one more self that Jesus talks about here. Not only the separated self of the Pharisee. And not only the swallowed self of the tax collector. But the self of the man who walks out of the temple that day lifted by the grace of God.

Remember, tomorrow he'll be back here again. How should he pray then? If he stands to thank God for his new-found righteousness, won't he be like the separated self of the Pharisee? And if he throws himself to the ground again and beats his chest in pious pain, how often can he swallow himself and still find himself?

That's why a new self has to take over. The see-through self. The self that no longer pays attention to either its strengths or its weaknesses. You may know about them. But you don't need to pay attention to them. G. K. Chesterton once said that our truest selves are like windows. They're meant to be transparent. Any evil in our lives is some form of dirt on the glass. It covers us over. It hides us. It portrays us in ways that are different from what we truly are. So with pride. It's a painting on the window of our hearts that calls attention to itself: See how beautiful I am! See how wonderful I am! And swallowing our pride is like washing that window. But it's not the washing nor the dirt that we should focus on. When the washing is done, the self that's left should walk away, oblivious to itself. Humiliation is no more godly than is pride. And the point of Jesus' parable is not that we should constantly berate ourselves, but that somewhere, by the grace of God, we find something bigger than ourselves on which to focus!

You know how it is. A young boy wanted to measure himself, to find out how tall he was. But he didn't have   a ruler. So he made one. And then he measured himself. Nine feet! Mommy! he shouted, I'm nine feet tall! But that's how it is when you measure yourself by your own ruler. The proud find themselves nine feet tall and look down on everyone else. The humiliated find themselves three feet tall and stare at the knees of everyone else.

But the self that's see-through merely looks beyond itself and walks the streets of life with grace.

How did Toscanini put it one time?! He was rehearsing with a great crowd of musicians--an orchestra and a chorus and a very famous and very temperamental soprano soloist. And she didn't mind it when he told the chorus how to sing. And she didn't mind it when he told the orchestra how to play. But she certainly did mind it when he tried to tell her how to express her part. She got more and more agitated with him. And finally she erupted. She shouted back at him: I am the star of this performance! But Toscanini just looked at her sadly. An then he said quietly, Madame, in this performance there are no stars! There's only the music!

Maybe that's what Isaac Watts had in mind when he wrote:

"When I survey the wondrous Cross
On which the Prince of Glory died,
My richest gain I count but loss
And pour contempt on all my pride."

Honor Roll
All Saints' Day
Hebrews 11:1-16; 11:32-12:3

Let me begin this morning with a few paragraphs from this little book. It's called *A Letter of Consolation*. It was written by Henri Nouwen to his father, six months after a death in the family. Listen to his words:

"Next Monday it will be half a year since mother died. It will be Holy Week and both of us will be preparing ourselves to celebrate Easter. How will this Easter be for us? You will be in the parish church of our little Dutch town listening to the story of Christ's resurrection. I will read that same story to monks and guests in a Trappist monastery in upstate New York. Both of us will look at the Easter candle, symbol of the risen Christ, and think not only of him but also of her. Our minds and hearts will be flooded with ideas and feelings that are too deep, too complex, and too intimate to express. But I am sure that we both shall think about last year's Easter when she was still with us. We both shall remember how she loved this great feast and how she decorated the house with flowers and the dinner table with purple and yellow ribbons. Somehow it seems long, long ago.

"Isn't that your experience also? The last six months could as well have been six years. Her death changed our experience of time; the short period between last October and this April seemed a very strange time in which the days, weeks, and months were as long as they were for a small child who is taking his first steps. We had to relearn life. Every 'normal' experience became for us like a new experience. It had the quality of a 'first time.' How often have we used these words! The first Christmas without Mother, the first New Year without Mother, the first wedding anniversary without Mother. And now it will be the first Easter without Mother. I know that you have been asking yourself often, as I have, 'How will it be without her?' We can hardly remember any of these events without her being part of them. We can no longer predict how we will feel on these familiar days and occasions. They are, in fact, no longer familiar. They have become suddenly aware how intimately our ideas, feelings, and perceptions were determined by her presence. Easter was not only an important day to celebrate, but a day to celebrate with her, a day on which her voice was heard, her letters anticipated, her active presence felt--so much so that we could not distinguish between the joys brought to us by the feast and the joys brought to us by her presence at the feast. They had become one and the same. But now we are forced to make a distinction, and now we have become like children who have to learn to do things for the first time on their own.

"New experiences such as these have made the last six months a strange time for us. Her death became an ongoing death for us. Every time we lived through another event without her, we felt her absence in a new way. We became aware of deep connections with her that we had forgotten for a while but that were brought back to consciousness by the forward movement of history. And each time, she died again in us. Memories of what she would have done, said, or written on certain occasions made us more aware of her not being with us and deepened our grief." (pp. 13-16)

Do you know what he's talking about? Have you spent time there with him? I know that many of you have.

Our deepest human need is for community. There's a hunger in our hearts for relationships. It's the greatest hunger we have. Do you know where our English word "crazy" comes from? It has its roots in the French word 'ecrase' which means broken and shattered. And that's why, sometimes, we go "crazy" with grief. A parent dies, and we feel suddenly so alone. A spouse dies, and our whole outlook on the world changes overnight. A child dies, and a part of us dies inside. Listen to these words from a parent who knows:

> "When a child dies," she writes,
> "your heart splits,
>   tears down the middle, right in two.
>   When a child dies, your soul is downcast,
>   your eyes seek a God afar off.
>   When a child dies, you feel low,
>   lower than you've ever been, the bottom.
>   When a child dies, your arms are empty,
>   dreams shattered, hopes in vain...
>   When a child dies, your burden is too heavy,
>   you stumble and teeter and finally fall...."

("When a Child Dies," Anne Childs)

Eric Wolterstorff died one afternoon in 1983. He was climbing the face of a mountain in Germany, and his foot slipped, and his hand missed its grip, and he plunged to his death. His father went to claim the body. When he got there, they handed him Eric's shoes. You know what? Eric's climbing shoes didn't have a single scratch on them! Here's Eric's body, smashed, bloody, beaten lifeless... But his shoes were bright and fresh. They looked like they were ready for another climb. Eric's father went sick inside. He wanted to call the people at the factory that made those shoes and tell them sarcastically that they should put this line in their advertisements: "Know that if you bump and scrape to death on a mountain, these shoes will come through and unscathed, ready to be worn again by family and friends!" Sick! Sick, sick, sick! That a young man should die and that his shoes should look so good! This is what his father wrote:

"There's a hole in the world now. In the place where he was, there's not just nothing. A center, like no other, of memory and hope and knowledge and affection which once inhabited this earth is gone. Only a gap remains. A perspective on this world unique in this world which once moved about within this world has been rubbed out. Only a void is left. There's nobody now who saw just what he saw, knows what he knew, remembers what he remembered, loves what he loved. A person, an irreplaceable person, is gone. Never again will anyone inhabit the world the way he did. Questions I have can never now get answers. The world is emptier. My son is gone. Only a hole remains, a void, a gap, never to be filled." ("Lament for a Son")

Therefore we must remember the dead. We have to remember the dead, don't we?! We have to remember them for a number of reasons.

For one thing, we have to remember them because they're part of our identity. Who are you? they ask us. And what do we say? Did we spring into this world by ourselves? Did we fashion our own shape, splice our own genes, create our own character? You know we didn't.

Virginia Stem Owens spends a summer in the little wooden shack that her grandfather built nearly two generations before. She listens to the stories of those who knew him. She hears the tales of his early days. She reads the reminisces of diaries and logs and journals. And what does she find? She finds that she's a lot like him! A man she never really knew! But there they are, two souls connected through space and time by some mysterious chains of DNA that linked his body to her body, that bound his heart to her heart, that shaped his mind like her mind, that locked his soul to her soul. She remembers him, and she remembers herself! She calls him to mind, and she finds an image she recognizes staring back from the mirror.

Someone once told the story of a little girl. She went into her bedroom and she found that the cleaning woman had knocked her doll to the floor. It was one of those old porcelain-faced dolls, the kind that shatter easily. And there was her doll on the floor, splintered a dozen ways. She cried over her doll, and the cleaning woman reprimanded her. "Don't cry!" she said, crossly. "You'll get over it! Your Mommy will get you another one!" How cruel! It did matter! Anybody who knows children knows that! This was <u>her</u> doll. Maybe her parents could get <u>another</u> doll. But they couldn't replace <u>this</u> one. And neither can we replace those who die.

The poet Tennyson felt so upset one time. It comes through, in his verse "In Memoriam." His best friend died. And then, at the funeral, someone had tossed this line off to him: Well, don't forget, this person said, you've still got other friends. Who cares! he says in his poem. Don't make him common! Just one of the crowd! As if another can step into his place! I need to remember him! His face! His eyes! His manners and habits! His speech and movements and wit and outlook! Don't take that away from me!

Four thousand years ago, says the historian, on a sunny afternoon in Egypt, heartbroken parents laid to rest in a carved sarcophagus the body of their beloved little daughter. A few years ago two English explorers discovered the tomb. They entered the cave that had been shut all that time, and they found the sarcophagus. And on it were inscribed these words in Hieroglyphics: "O my life, my love, my little one! Would to God I had died for you!" Those two explorers took the hats off their heads in that moment, and in silence they stood there in the darkness. Then they left the cool sanctuary of the cave, and they sealed the entrance. They hid it so that no one might ever find it again. For grief like that deserves its privacy. Let no one make light of my grief when someone near to me dies.

There's a second reason why we have to remember the dead. **Sometimes it's because they have hurt us so tragically.** Think of Simon Wiesenthal. He was a successful architect in Europe. Two university degrees in engineering. Only wanted to live quietly with his family and create beautiful buildings. Then the Gestapo came in 1943. They arrested him at his home. They killed 89 of his relatives. His wife's mother was shot to death on the stairway of her house. He watched helplessly while the Nazis crammed his own mother into a freight car, loaded beyond description with hundreds of elderly Jewish women. She perished with thousands of them in the Belzec "showers." Wiesenthal was shipped from one concentration camp to another. When the Allied troops liberated Mauthausen in February of 1945, he was one of the few human scarecrows that stumbled out of the gate. Since the end of the war, Wiesenthal operates the Jewish Documentation Centre in Vienna. No one must forget! he says. No one must forget!

Four weeks ago I was on the telephone with a man in Woodstock. He was a Dutch immigrant to Canada following World War II. Now he lives a life of religious service. At least that's what he calls it. He goes around speaking to groups, any that will have him, about the conspiracy of the Illuminati... about the false hoax of the Holocaust... about the cruel lie people have been besmirching on the good name of Adolph Hitler... And my blood boils. And I hang up the telephone. I don't want to talk to this man anymore. Somebody has to remember! Somebody has to keep count! Somebody has to set the record straight!

It happens on a personal level too. Last summer, when I spoke at a conference in Hamilton, a woman came up to me with tears in her eyes. I had asked them, as a group, to bring back memories of childhood, to recall scenes from their parental homes. And she said to me: You hurt me today! She said: I haven't got any good memories of my childhood! She said: I've kept these things hidden all these years, and now you make me bring them up! And we talked for awhile about her memories. And then she said that she wasn't really angry with me. She said that more than anything she was afraid. She was afraid, because she saw the way she had pushed people away, all her life. She was afraid, because she saw what was happening between herself and her daughter. She was afraid, because she knew that if she didn't deal with her memories soon, they would eat her alive, and they would destroy everything good she still had in her life. Her father died long ago. But he still controlled her mind and her body like he did when she was young.

She has to remember him, like Wiesenthal has to remember the Nazis, because they took something so important away. They robbed these people of dignity. They robbed these people of personality. They robbed these people of a sense of goodness, and fair play, and love. And no one has a right to do that and get away with it!!!

There's a third reason why we have to remember the dead. **Sometimes it's because they have challenged us so movingly.** That's what this 11th chapter of Hebrews is all about, isn't it? I remember when I first really read it. I was in Grade 6 at the time. Our teacher was Mr.

Lobbes. It was the first time we had a male teacher in school. And we didn't really like him. He was too stern, too tough, too strict. But one day we sat there in class. It was right about this time of the year: the end of October, the beginning of November. And he was telling us about Martin Luther and the start of the great Protestant Reformation of the church. And then he said how important it was to remember the heroes of the past. The people who made a difference in life. The people who showed us what courage and caring and conviction were all about. And he had us open our Bibles to Hebrews chapter 11. And then he asked us to do something that horrified me at the time. He asked us to take our pens and to write in our Bibles at the top of the chapter: Heroes of Faith. And then he read through the chapter out loud: slowly, somberly, significantly. And we heard the names of those who believed in God. And we heard what a difference it made in their lives. And we heard the litany of what they were able to do, by the strength of faith, and by the courage of conviction. I'll never forget Mr. Lobbes reading this chapter. And I'll never forget the scrawled handwriting at the top of Hebrews 11 in my old King James Bible: Heroes of Faith!

We all need heroes. Heroes remind us of the rest of life, of the stuff that we can be if we stand on their shoulders, of the potential in the human spirit for good, when God's spirit flows through it.

The great missionary Stanley Jones once told of a woman in Australia. Her two daughters were missionaries in China. One day, during riots and political upheaval, roving bands of thugs came through and murdered her two daughters. She was 62 years old at the time. And when the funerals were over people expected her to shrivel up and die. But not this woman. She was made of heroic stuff. She went instead to China. To the

101

city where her daughters had worked. To the house where her daughters had lived. To the place where they had died cruelly. And she learned the language. And she served the people. And she taught the love of Christ. And she died at the age of 82, still in China, loved by the people who had killed her daughters! They buried her body there, next to the two graves of her children. Dr. Jones used to say: there's a person who needs to be remembered! And he was right!

When Plato told of the death of Socrates in his dialogues, he says: "...it seemed as if we were going to lose a father and to be orphans for the rest of our life." He closes off the tale like this: "Such was the end...of our friend, a man, I think, who was the wisest and justest, and the best man I have ever known." And Plato wrote the story of Socrates knowing that those who remembered him would be the better for it.

And how do we do that? It was only two years ago this month that Pastor Peter showed us what a good thing remembering can be. He stood in the pulpit of the Jarvis Christian Reformed Church, and he lifted out of history the memories of his mother and his father. This is All Saints' Day. And you can be sure that he's passing those two saints across the window screens of his mind more than once today.

I remember my Grandfather today. I can still see him sitting at the kitchen table, in their retirement home, slicing a raw onion with a paring knife, and eating it section by section! Never have worms if you eat a good onion now and again! he said. That's just one moment of his life that's part of my treasury today.

Last spring I told you that my old buddy Lowell Freiborg was sick. He had leukemia. Lowell died this past summer. Not a great saint nor a great sinner. But he was part of my life. And I remember him today.

How do we use All Saints' Day to our profit? I think the first verses of Hebrews 12 point us in the right direction. Here we are, says the author, surrounded by this great cloud of witnesses. It's like we're in a huge coliseum, a stadium like the Skydome, and it's a sell-out crowd! 50,000 people packing the place! Full right up to the nose-bleed seats, hanging from the rafters. And we're jogging along. It's the final lap of the Marathon. And none of us really has the energy to make it to the finish line. Then, says the author of Hebrews, you have to look around you. You have to go to church on All Saints' Day, and catch sight of the crowds in the stands. And you have to do two things.

On the one hand, you have to distill the best out of the past. You have to catch the meaning of all those lives. You have to find the purpose to the generations that went before you. If you are, indeed, linked by more than fate or chance to those who have died, then the meaning of your life has to be linked, as well, to the meaning of theirs. If they had a race to run, you have a race to run. If they had a purpose to fulfill, you have a purpose to fulfill. If they had a reason for their existences, you have a reason for your existence.

Tony Campolo tells it so well in one of his stories. He's a member of a Baptist church in Philadelphia. And every year, on the Sunday between Christmas and New Year's, they have what they call "Student Recognition Day." They get all the students who are home for the holidays to come up to the front of the church and to tell a little bit about what they're doing and what they're learning. And that way the whole congregation catches up on the news, and they show how they're all in this thing called life together. And then, says Tony, the Senior Pastor comes along, and he marches up and own in front of that row of students. And he says a few words to them. And one year he said something like this. He said: "Children, you're going to die!" He said: "You may not think you're going to die. But you're going to die! One of these days, they're going to take you out to the cemetery, drop you in a hole, throw some dirt on your face, and go back to the church and eat potato salad." He said: "When you were born, you were the only one who was crying. Everybody else was happy. The important question I want to ask is this: When you die, are you the only one who will be happy and leave everybody else crying?!" He said: "The answer depends on whether you live to get titles, or you live to get testimonies. When you die, will they stand around reciting fancy titles that you earned, or are they going to stand around giving testimonies of the good things you did for them? Will they list your degrees and awards, or will they tell about what a blessing you were to them? Will you leave behind just a newspaper column telling people how important you were, or will you leave crying people who give testimonies of how they've lost the best friend they ever had?" He said: "There's nothing wrong with titles. Titles are good things to have. But if it ever comes down to a choice between a title or a testimony--go for the testimony!" And then, says Tony, he did one of those good, old-fashioned, Black Baptist poetic "rips." He started off at the beginning of the Bible, and he brought together every pair that's listed there. He swayed in the pulpit, and he waved his finger, and he did in person what Hebrews 11 does so well on paper. He said: "Pharaoh may have had a title... But Moses had a testimony!" He said: "Nebuchadnezzar may have had a title... But Daniel had a testimony!" He said: "Queen Jezebel may have had a title... But Elijah had the testimony!" And he went right on through the Old Testament, till he came up with this one, the one they were all waiting for. He shouted:

Pilate may have had a title... And the church erupted with faith. The whole congregation roared back at him: But Jesus had the testimony!

That's the start of it, isn't it?! That's why these lives are played out on the screen, in glimpses of color. They didn't all have titles... But every one of them had a testimony! And that's why they mean something to you! And that's why the saints in your life mean something to you. And that's why you have to remember them today.

But here's the other side of it. **We're told that we've also got to get free of the weights that entangle us, and the sins that trip us up.** And that's where All Saints' Day plays a part as well. Because you can't run with a testimony when your heart is pounded by evil memories. Gwendolyn Carr, whose daughter-in-law committed suicide, penned these lines. She said:

"Old wounds often split their seams,
and spill the festering out
from where the healing's certainty
hides nagging doubt;
from where the shiny covering,
that smooth contented place,
harbors in its hollow
some discontented trace."

And she's right. Unresolved pains from former relationships live on in frustration especially after one of the parties dies. And sinners who've hurt us, and loved ones who've died too soon, and friends who never finished what they started with us, have got to be released.

In a recent issue of *Perspectives*, a woman who calls herself Kathi Carino tells in powerful ways how she was abused by her father. She grew up in a very wonderful Christian home, at least from all outward appearances. But behind closed doors, and in secret rooms, her father used to do to her unmentionable things. But here's the part that's important for us today. For a long while, she functioned in society in ways that betrayed no hurt. Stoically, she says, she blocked that part of her life out. It didn't exist. It wouldn't affect her. She couldn't let it get her down. She thought she had it all under control. But monsters are monsters, and they lurk in our shadows no matter how hard we try to imagine them away. And finally the tortures of the past threatened her marriage and her relationship with her four children. Left to herself she would have ended it all. But her husband helped her find a counselor. And her counselor helped her go through the white-water rapids of her horrible past. "And there," she says, "each new memory...feels like my soul is crashing against a sub-merged rock...there have been times," she says, "when I believed I would drown in the pain." "And then," she says, "I read the book of Hebrews. And I heard of the Jesus who runs the race of life with me. And I saw his picture looming out of the mists just ahead. And he calls me on. And he knows my pain. And he points me to a place where the hurt can be healed. And I find myself cheered on by my husband, and by my children, and by my friends. And All Saints' Day means something new to me."

Hebrews chapter 11 is the Honor Roll of the Church. It's the beginning of the Honor Roll we should read today, on All Saints' Day. We need to read it, not because it has some magical, mystical powers. But we need to read it because we do not stand alone in time. An old Latin proverb said: One man is no man at all. How true!

Who are the Saints who have made you what you are? Remember them today!

"When he runs he never wearies
When he walks he never faints
He is striving for the Master
and cheered on by the saints
Earthly runners may be weary
But a better race is on
Won't you come and join the runners
Maranatha marathon." --William Walston Hew

Dance in the Desert
Isaiah 35

The story comes from yesterday's newspaper. A country torn by strife. Warring factions raiding the villages. Plagues and famine sweeping the country. Food is gone, and the children starve.

Is it Somalia? Yes, and Ethiopia and Bangladesh and Kurdistan and a hundred other wastelands on our globe.

And it's Judah, too. Little Judah, squatting on the southern slopes of Palestine. Judah is all that remains of the once proud people of God. Nothing much to be proud about anymore. The world is a rough-house of beer-drinking bullies. Every day another by-stander gets beat to a pulp. Every night another orphaned child crawls into a creepy corner, kept awake by the unholy trinity: cold, and hunger, and fear.

Isaiah doesn't even report the big stories any-more. The conflict between the superpowers is old news. What's there to say today that hasn't been flaunted nauseously before. News is only news when people tune it in. But this world has grown small with pain, and every eye is turned in suspicion toward others who cower like me. This is what the worst of the classic orphanage is all about. Try to talk of important things, like politics and religion, in a place like that, and you find your words swallowed up in the din of cries and torment and pain.

It's bedlam in Palestine. You know where the word "bedlam" comes from, don't you? There was a hospital in London, England, called the Hospital of St. Mary of Bethlehem. Over the years it became a poor person's last home, a final stop on death's road. Then it was used to collect those who no longer fit into society. They called it an insane asylum. And the noise of weeping and wailing shrieked out of the place all day long. Till the hospital was known by its din. And they talked of Bethlehem over and over in the city, and the great grief there. And it wasn't long before the name was shortened, and the meaning changed: Bedlam! The mighty roar of hopeless pain.

And the world still knows what bedlam is about. A couple of years ago the newspaper on a university campus ran a contest. The editors offered a prize for the best definition of the word "life." Here's what they got. One said: Life is a joke that isn't funny! Another pointed to the children and quipped: Life is a jail sentence which we get for the crime of being born. And someone summed it up like this: Life is a disease for which the only cure is death.

Devastation

That's the picture behind our reading this morning. The superpowers are still at it: Assyria and Babylon and Syria. But on the fringes of the far-flung fury and fighting, little Judah is hiding from the rocks that cousin Edom is throwing. These two are always at it, aren't they? Remember Jacob and Esau?

Twin brothers? Taunting one another? Scuffing in the dust? Well, Judah is all that's left of Jacob. And Edom is all that's left of Esau. And the story of Isaiah 34 and 35 is told in other brush-strokes by the prophet Obadiah.

You see, Edom and Judah are like orphans fighting in the middle of a crowd of big people. All around them ring the power-brokers of society. And they throw down bets while these two scrap. And they taunt them on with vicious stabs and cruel jokes. And scrawny Edom whips whimpering Judah into a corner.

What do you do when you've been pushed into that corner? What do you do when you're all alone, when life crowds you like a bully, and you sit on your thin mattress in the cancer ward?

One fellow tells this story. He started as a volunteer in the children's wards at a hospital. Burn victims. Deformities. Terminal cancer. So much pain! So many tears! Somebody has to bring a little cheer, he thought. So he got one of those clown's noses: a bright red foam ball. And someone gave him a pair of oversized shoes. And then he painted his face, and he pulled on a wig. And he went to work the next day like that. And some of the children were scared of him. An some were captivated. And some began to smile a little, for the first time in ages. But some couldn't stop crying. The pain. The agony. The loneliness. What to do with them?! So the next day the clown brought along some popcorn. An when he came to the side of a crying child, he took a kernel of popcorn, and he placed it gently against the cheek, and he soaked up the cascading tears with its fluff. And then he popped that kernel into his mouth.

It was a stroke of genius, he said. A gift given to him by God. The only time some of those children stopped crying was the moment they knew that somebody else cared enough to eat their tears!

That's the hope of this moment, this scene of laughter in Isaiah 35. Chapter 34 gushes with tears. But, says the prophet, look! Someone's coming to the cancer ward this morning! Someone's coming to eat your tears! Someone's coming to take away the pain!

Deliverance

In the last century there was an artist who loved the prophecies of Isaiah. His name was Edward Hicks. You've seen one of his creations, recently, if you read any magazines at all. There's a very famous company here in Canada that's made use of his classic work, "The Peaceable Kingdom" in their present ad campaign. You know, the one where the page is covered with animals, beasts great and ferocious. And there, walking in the middle of them, is a young child. It's the scene that Isaiah describes several times over, a scene that fits also with this picture, in chapter 35. Desert wastes. Howling beasts. A world in chaos. And then, a miracle comes from God to turn it all round to peace. What you may not know is this: Edward Hicks spent his entire life trying to get that scene just right. Early in his career, the animals look tame and almost silly on his canvas, like stuffed toys in the little boy's bedroom. But the longer Hicks lived, and the older he got, the more restless his portraits of "The Peaceable Kingdom" got, as well. The animals grew larger. Their eyes got darker. The expressions on their faces became more sultry, more ferocious. And the miracle of all these wilderness enemies resting together became more and more incredible.

You see, Hicks actually believed at one time that he would live to see the day when world peace would come, when nations would beat their swords to ploughshares, and when children would sleep at night in security. But as Hicks watched the political climates unfold, as he read his morning newspaper, as he counted the casualties of cruelty, he knew that it would never happen without a miracle.

By the end of his life he had painted "The Peaceable Kingdom" more than 80 times, each edition darker and more ominous. And he said, in his final year, that he still didn't get it right. But this one thing he never did either: he never took the child out of the picture. He never took the child out of the picture.

Dance

Sometimes theology doesn't communicate very well. I think of that each week as I study at my desk for you, reading commentaries, digging through deep doctrinal dissertations. I learn much. I think I know a little bit more each year about the mysteries of God and life and the healing of the soul. It's only a taste, mind you. And it seems that the more I taste, the thirstier I get.

But here's another thing I know as well. I know that when God wants to communicate most to me, He does it not through dogma or proposition, but through picture and through story.

And that picture, at the heart of Isaiah's prophecies, is a haunting one. The child among the animals. The tiny wisp of a person, nearly crushed by these big bodies. And yet, whenever Isaiah tells the story, whenever he paints the picture, it's always the child that he highlights. Not the jaws nor the claws. Not the talons nor the felons. Not the aggression nor the depression. But the child. The child. The wee promise of God set down right in the middle of all this milling madness.

There's a children's story book that shows it so well. It's called *Dance in the Desert*. It's the story of a young woman and her husband. They're on a journey. It's a journey through the wilderness, in a caravan bound for Egypt. The desert places are ominous, alive with ferocious wild beasts. Everyone in the caravan is nervous. They know that sleep will settle uneasily over the camp tonight, when the world belongs to eyes that glow in the dark. So twilight comes, and they build a great bonfire, hoping to drive back the shadows. And suddenly they start, because a great lion appears. The mother reaches for her child. She must snatch him to safety. But what happens?! The child holds out his arms to the lion! And the lion lifts his front paws, and he hops around on his hind legs! Look! He's dancing! And then, from the desert, come running several little mice, and two donkeys, and a snake, and a couple of clumsy ostriches! And three great eagles swoop in from the purple skies! And on the other side of the camp a unicorn emerges, and a pelican, and even two dragons. And they all bow before the child, and they all dance together round and round him as he stands in the center of their great circle, laughing with delight.

And you know the name of that Child. You know how his face can never be erased from all those pictures, those pictures of the deserts of the world, those portraits of the wildernesses you walk. Somehow, under the shadowed skies of night, he tames the beasts that bother you. Somehow he makes the deserts sing. Somehow he puts to rest the warring of the nations, and even the sick skirmishings of Edom and Judah. The wilderness remains. But it's power is harnessed for peace.

I hesitate to add much to the picture. For some, I know I could never explain enough to make it real for you. And for others, you've already slipped quietly away from me, searching your souls for the place where the beasts and the night and the desert and the child come together around the fire.

Let me only add this one story. It's told by one of the master story-tellers of our age: Frederick Buechner. He tells of his personal travels through the wilderness of life. He calls it *The Sacred Journey*. And near the end is this scene. He sits at his mother's apartment one evening. They have supper together, in candlelight. But the telephone rings, jarringly, as it sometimes does. And it's the beginning of a very bleak time for him. It's his friend on the other end, a friend from work. He's at the airport. His mother and father and pregnant sister were in an accident. They probably won't live. He's catching a plane to get to their hospital bedsides. Could Fred come to him at the airport and help him though this thing?

But Fred can't. He can't because he's afraid of the wilderness. He's scared of the beasts out there, and the demons of pain and cruelty. And so he sits by the flickering flames on the dinner table, hoping, with his mother, to shut out the howling of the animals. But it can't be done. Fred finds he can't write like he wants to. And he can't find another job. And his uncle won't take him into his advertising business. And he falls in love with a woman who doesn't love him. And every way in the canyons of New York seems to be the way of death for him.

But one Sunday he goes to church. He's not a Christian, he knows. But what else is there to do on a Sunday morning?! And it's George Buttrick in the pulpit, crafting images, weaving spells of pain and hope, grief and greatness. It's the story of Jesus in the desert. In the wilderness. In the place of great suffering, great pain, great temptation. And Jesus is tempted there by Satan, says Buttrick; tempted to find a way out of the desert, tempted to give up his torment in exchange for fame and for wealth and for power. But Jesus refuses the crown of Satan, says Buttrick. He refuses it because it offers too little. And there, says Buttrick, in the wilderness, Jesus becomes king in another way. For those who wander in the deserts with him gather around him. And somehow, says Buttrick, they know that he can tame their beasts too.

And here's the moment that dug into Buechner's soul. Because Buttrick said that the moment of truth was the moment when each wilderness wanderer got rid of his own wretched crown and placed it in the hand of Jesus. What happens in that moment? Three things, said Buttrick: confession and tears and great laughter.

Confession he could understand. Tears he had shed enough of. But great laughter? How could that be? What was there to laugh about in the desert? He wasn't sure at the time. But little by little it dawned on him. The beasts would never lie silent next to one another. Edom and Judah would forever be throwing punches. Children in Somalia would always be waiting for food. And Bedlam would always come out of Bethlehem.

But so too would the Child. The Child who would stand among the beasts and soothe them. The Child who would stand among the nations and quiet them. The Child who would clap his hands in the desert night and call for the dancing to begin.

Mountain Standard Time
Advent
Isaiah 2:1-5

Somewhere today there's a widow who sits at the window of her apartment. Her body is motionless, her hands rest quietly in her lap, her eyes don't even blink. She stares into space, not really noticing the bits and pieces of life that flutter around in a frenzy out beyond the glass barrier. She's lost in the world of her thoughts. In her mind, you see, she's a young girl again. She romps with her best friend through fields of flowers. She whispers secrets into her mother's ear. She feels the caress of her lover's hand on her skin, and the heat of passion surges through her veins.

Somewhere today there's a man on a business trip away from home. It's Sunday, and he's stuck in a distant motel. His only companion is the television. He flicks from channel to channel. And here's an old movie. He's seen it before. But it captures his mind again, and he's caught in a trance. "The Man from Snowy River." That's what it's called. "The Man from Snowy River." It's a story of love and courage, of strength and bravery, of gentleness and humility... And long before the final scenes fade into music, he's crying. He's crying and he's crying and he's crying.... Why? Because something inside his soul just called to him. He's not sure what it is. But he knows that it's the best of him. And whatever he's become, whatever it was that brought him to this place on business, it's not what he wanted his life to be all about. He's lost something along the way. Because he forgot that Voice. And he followed a different path.

Somewhere today there's a young bride who sits on a hard church bench. Out of the corner of her eye she sees her husband. She can hardly keep from grinning!

She didn't know that she could love someone so much! Who is this powerful stranger who's suddenly become her life, her laughter, her love? The service of worship swirls around her, but she hears little of what is said, and she knows even less of what is done. Yet when they rise to sing, the words are all her prayer: "Love divine, all loves excelling, Joy of Heaven, to earth come down! Fix in us thy humble dwelling; All thy faithful mercies crown!"

Somewhere today there's a police officer cruising the back streets of the city. Not much happening. Nice to have things quiet. The radio plays softly in the background, one of those "golden oldies" weekend shows. He drives past a park and stops to watch the children play. Four of them: Asian, White, Native, and Black. And the radio catches his attention. Because Dion is singing. He's singing a ballad of great grace and of great pain. It's one that climbed the charts decades ago not because of its funky beat, but because of its mournful cry for three lost brothers: Abraham, Martin, and John. That's the name of the song. Those are the people he sings of. Three men who spoke of righteousness, and of justice, and of liberty. Three leaders of nations who were stopped cold by assassins' bullets. And suddenly this man remembers why it was that he went to police academy. And he wants to run up to those four children, and he wants to gather them into his arms, and he wants to breathe a blessing of hope on their heads, and he wants to tell them that they hold the key to the future of the human race in their playing hands.

Do you know these people? Do you know what they're feeling? Do you know what makes them one, what makes their faces come alive in your mind, what makes them real to you? It's Mountain Standard Time.

You see, we're all bound by time. Time is our teacher. Time is our boss. Time is our constant companion. Time locks us into the march of life, and forces us to wake up each morning in a place we've never been before, in a place we can never return to again. And all our lives we struggle with time. When will we ever have enough time? When will I be old enough? When will time stop long enough for me to love you? One woman went through a great period of depression when her husband died. The grief slowed time for her. A year later, somewhat recovered, she talked with her pastor. How long did it last for you, he asked, these months of loneliness in the wilderness of your grief? This is what she told him. She said: Longer than I had hoped, but not as long as I had feared! Bound by time! She wrestled alone in the deserts with him, captive to his march of dictation. Wilderness Standard Time. The time of struggle. The time of depression. The time of empty hands.

Time marches on, we say. Business Standard Time. The time of racing and pacing. The time of timeclocks and punchcards. The time of shiftwork and overtime. The time of hiring and firing, of corporate climbs and trembling takeovers. Someone tells of a young man who'd just gotten his diploma. He was so excited! He rushed out of the graduation ceremonies, and he took his piece of paper, and he held it up to the skies, and he said: Here I am, World!! I've got my B.A.!! And a large voice boomed back at him from the heavens: Stick around, son, and I'll teach you the rest of the alphabet! That's what happens in Business Standard Time, doesn't it? We learn our paces. We march to the corporate drumbeat.

And then there's Relational Standard Time. The poet puts it this way: When as a child I laughed and wept, Time crept. He says: When as a youth I dreamt and talked, Time walked. He says: When I became a full-grown man, Time ran. He says: When older still I daily grew, Time flew. You know what he's talking about, don't you? The time that flies when you're having fun. The time that races and teases and stalls and hurries. The time that lingers during the week, but rushes through a Friday night. The time that charts the weeks of courtship, and organizes the plans for the wedding. The time that counts nine months meticulously in pregnancy, and steps year-by-year through the grades of school. The time that changes babies into children, and children into teens, and teens into young adults, and young adults into newlyweds, and newlyweds into parents, and parents into middle-aged folk, and middle-aged folk into seniors. Relational Standard Time.

But there comes a moment in all our lives when it's Mountain Standard Time that we long for. It's a moment when the time zones we've lived in don't promise enough, anymore. It's an hour when the clocks on our walls and the watches on our wrists and the chronometers in our cars can't tell us everything we need to know about the aging of our lives. And somewhere in time we long to step into eternity.

There's an old Star Trek program that holds a neat picture. Those of you who are Trekkies will remember it. It's the one where a race of people invades the starship Enterprise, but no one can see them, because they live in a different dimension of time. Their systems respond to a different clock. So while all the crew of the Enterprise carry on with life in their own time-frame, these beings dance around them as if they weren't moving at all. They romp and roam the ship, and celebrate their freedom in a land of time-bound bodies. And they're only detected when one woman, who kind of likes Captain Kirk, slips a pill into his coffee so that his body system accelerates, and he's able to enter the world of her time zone.

Perhaps that's the kind of thing Isaiah has in mind, when he pens this picture for his people. They're so busy with the world of their time zones, some caught up in the rush of Business Standard Time, some wasting away in Wilderness Standard Time. But there's going to come a day, he says, when Someone will drop a pill into your morning coffee, and your systems will enter a new time zone, and you'll look at your watches and you'll find everything moving now in Mountain Standard Time. And here you'll learn again the meaning of your lives. And here you'll see again the purpose of your times. And here you'll find again the strength of your hearts and the beauty of your souls and the wisdom of your minds. For in the world of Mountain Standard Time, the pace is set by the King of the Mountain, the One who measures all time correctly, and the One before whom all Time bows as a servant.

In the weeks of Advent we mark time. We mark time like Isaiah marked time. Waiting, in anticipation, for our Lover to come along and drop the seed of eternity into our morning coffee, and quicken the pace of our heartbeats, and stretch out the span of our moments. Of course, those who know already the King on the Mountain live with moments of eternity pacing their days.

I thought of that last week. My parents called. They just returned from three weeks of travel to Australia and New Zealand. How was it?! I asked. Wonderful!! they said. But boy! Was it hard to keep up with the changing time zones! Their bodies wanted to remain on Minnesota time while their spirits tried to live on the other side of the International Date Line. To the traveler, that's a tough business.

But to the citizen of the Kingdom of Heaven, it's a tough business too. Because once we've tasted life on the other side of the International Date Line, even if we live in Minnesota, or in Ontario, or in Siberia, the pace of our existence quickens to the ticking of that other clock. And we who march to the beat of Wilderness Standard Time, of Business Standard Time, or Relational Standard Time, find our spirits torn by another timeframe. We find our souls yearning for another pace of existence, and another measure of life. And Advent makes us restless to live again on the Mountain. On God's Mountain. In Mountain Standard Time.

That's why the widow's body allows her soul to slip back to Mountain Time memories. That's why the businessman's soul searches for Mountain Time meaning that he lost somewhere along the way in Business Standard Time. That's why Relational Standard Time can't capture all the thrill of the young bride's soul; she's lifted her heart to Mountain Standard Time. That's why the police officer searches for the Mountain of racial justice to climb when he sees the children at play. Sometime Mountain Standard Time, God's time, will make them brothers forever!

Do you know why you came here this morning? Do you know why you came to this church, and wanted to become a member of it? It's because there's something of Mountain Standard Time that whistles through this place. We're bound by the clock across the street, that chimes the quarter hour in Eastern Standard Time. But just for awhile, in this place of worship, we experience the quickening pace of life on the mountain of God somewhere beyond the International Date Line. And Mountain Standard Time becomes our wish, and our hope, and our prayer.

A Tale of Two Tables
Communion
Isaiah 25

Let me tell you a little story this morning, and it'll help you understand this short passage from Isaiah's prophecy. The Chinese tell of a man who died, and his spirit was winged away by the angels. On the way to heaven, though, they made a little detour. They took a side trip to hell. The angels said, We do this with everybody. It makes them appreciate heaven even more. So here they were at the windows of hell. And the man wasn't so sure that he was in the right place. Because hell was lined with long tables, stretching off to the horizon. And on those tables was the best of every food he could think of: fresh fruits, the choicest cuts of meat, rich sauces and gravies, vegetables all simmered to perfection...It was every bit a feast fit for a king! And this was supposed to be hell! Heaven should be so good! But then his eyes were distracted by the crowds that thronged the tables. What a bunch! Bickering and arguing and fighting and pushing and shoving each other! It was like the scrimmage line of a football game. The man looked more closely at them. What a shock! Here were all these people sitting at tables overflowing with good things to eat, and yet every one of them was starving! Hollow eyes, sunken cheeks, ribs like washboards on every chest, knobby elbows and knees, where the muscles had wasted away...These folks were dying of hunger! How could it be?! What was going on?! So he asked his guide: What's the deal?! Why don't they eat?! Why are they all starving?! And the angel said to him, There's only one rule here in hell: they can eat all they want, but they have to use 4-foot chopsticks! The man looked again. Sure enough! All the people were picking at the food on the tables. But they couldn't get it to their mouths! The chopsticks were too long! What a nasty way to live! And even though their bodies were wasting away, they never died!

It was like the old Greek stories of Tantalus. He was the one who stole the nectar of the gods, and they punished him like this: they bound his feet to the bottom of a great river, so that just his head was sticking out. The waters swirled around his chin. And then they bewitched the waters, so that every time Tantalus bent down to drink, the waters flowed away from him! All that water, but never a drop to drink. The gods did another thing: they set Tantalus in the river right under the branches of a fruit tree. But here again, every time he stretched his fingers for something to eat, the wind blew the fruit out of his reach. Tantalized! That's the word we use! It comes from his name.

And here's the man at the windows of hell. Long tables burgeoning with good food. But all just out of reach because of those four-foot chopsticks. The maddening crowd of hell. Tantalized, but never satisfied.

The man shuddered. And the angels took to flight again. They winged him on his way to heaven. But here's the surprise of the story! Because, when they got to the gates of heaven, the man stopped them! He didn't want to go in! You know why? Because he looked through the doorway and all he saw were long rows of tables! Stretching to eternity! Loaded with good food! And seated on either side of every table were millions and millions and millions of folks. And in their hands were four-foot chopsticks! No! he said. Don't leave me here! Don't torture me this way! But the angels said, Look again! And then he noticed it. All these people looked happy, and well-fed, and delighted about their circumstances...! It was unbelievable! Their cheeks shone!

Their bellies were full! Their faces were rosy and expressive! Laughter! Conversation! Not a cross word or a bickering argument in the place! What's the deal?! he asked. What's going on?! And this is what his guide said. He said: Here we feed each other! Here we feed each other!

A tale of two tables. A story of two places, as far away as hell and heaven. How did Charles Dickens put it in his novel?

"It was the best of times,
it was the worst of times,
it was the age of wisdom,
it was the age of foolishness,
it was the epoch of belief,
it was the epoch of incredulity,
it was the season of Light,
it was the season of Darkness,
it was the spring of hope,
it was the winter of despair,
we had everything before us,
we had nothing before us,
we were all going direct to Heaven,
we were all going direct the other way...."

A Tale of Two Cities. And here, A Tale of Two Tables. Each one belongs to a different city. Each one belongs to a different kingdom.

Isaiah pictured them, in the passage we read this morning. A world in turmoil. Nations in conflict. And people scrounging at tables overloaded with food. But most are stuffing themselves in gluttony. Because that's what they've learned from the top. Their rulers, their kings, their leaders are gluttons. The purpose of power is consumption. Eat the other nations up, like Saddam Hussein ate up Kuwait, like the Europeans ate up the Native Peoples of North America, like the powers of the

First World eat up the countries of the Third World. And the feasting becomes maddening, till the gluttons of the nations have devoured each other several times over. And everybody wants. And everybody needs. And everybody takes. And every society becomes a culture of vampires. And the world grows very dark. And the nations run with blood. And the feasting tables grow heavy with booty. But it's never enough. And the eyes of the people grow mean. And their cheeks burn with anger. And their tongues lash out in rage. It looks like hell!

But wait! says Isaiah. Look! There's another table being laid! It's a feast of extravagance! It's a culinary delight! It's a showpiece of haute cuisine! And what's the difference? The difference is merely this: At the other tables of the nations the Kings are served first! In fact, the purpose of the tables is to collect from others in order to give to the Kings! That's the gluttony of the world order! That's the glut in the economic system. But here it's the King who sets the table as a gift for others! He doesn't suck it all to himself, like a giant vacuum cleaner. In fact, he serves at the table, giving food to the lowest, and the last, and the least. To the child who's too weak to raise a bottle to her lips. To the man who's arms were shot off in the War of the Worlds. To the woman who's elbows twist wildly away, pinned by torment and cruel beatings. The King sets the table. And it's a table of Grace. And no one feeds himself or herself. They are all fed by others, from the least of them to the greatest. And the atmosphere changes. And the sense of community spirit is made new. And those who have received from this King gain strength to feed others. And the table grows, till it stretches to eternity. And the food multiplies. And the feasting flourishes. And in that awful dark room of Hell, torn by the gluttonous slurping of demons, a little glimmer of light shines, and all Heaven breaks through.

Do you need a moral this morning?! Do you need a word of application?! Listen to this note from Frederick Buechner. He writes it in his novel *Love Feast*. He tells it in his story about Leo Bebb. Leo Bebb decides not to make a Thanksgiving dinner for himself that year. Instead, he makes a Thanksgiving meal for all who would come: the poor and hungry, the rich and hungry, the down-and-outer hungry, the up-and-inner hungry, the out-of-fashion hungry, and the fashionable hungry... You get the picture. And when they're at the table, Leo says this to them. He says: The kingdom of heaven is like a great feast...a love feast where no one is a stranger.

Why did you come here this morning? Do you know? What was this table that you sat at? Did you figure it out? Who stood at the head of the table? I mean the one who set it in the first place, long ago. Did he demand that you bring something to him to feed his gluttonous face? Or did he set the table for you? And call you to himself? And serve you with his chopsticks? And fill that void of hunger in your life?

This table expands, you know. It expands to the horizons of our society. It expands to the far reaches of London. It expands to the distant corners of Canada. It expands to the ends of the earth. And either you grab at its goodies with four-foot chopsticks and starve to spiritual death in the shadow of heaven, or you feed someone else with your four-foot chopsticks, because you've learned the heart of the King who called you to his table this morning.

A Tale of Two Tables. Do you know which one you're at?

Pain's Volcano
Numbers 20:1-13

Why did Moses strike the rock? Think about it. Here he was, 120 years old! Don't you think he'd learn to control his temper by this time? Sure, the Israelites were a cantankerous bunch! They were enough to make anybody a little angry! And besides that, the desert sun never stopped blazing! The heat put people on edge! And the hunger: never enough to eat, never enough to drink...You try staying sane when you're dying of exhaustion and starvation at the same time! And then try leading these people--Canadians are bad enough! A week ago, Friday night, the London Symphonic Orchestra & Chorus gave a great performance over at Centennial Hall. And the narrator for the evening had some marvelous quotes about Canadians. But this was the best: Canadians, she said, are people who carry moderation to an extreme! I like that! But now think of these people, these Israelites: bicker, bicker, bicker! That's all they ever seem to do! Well, maybe Moses has a right to get angry with them!

SMACK! SMACK! He whacks his staff against the rock! And God says, Moses, Moses, Moses...What am I going to do with you?!

You see, what makes this little story so fascinating is that it's not really like Moses to blow up this way! He's not usually an angry man! He's not a person who erupts with rage easily! Maybe he was earlier in his life. After all, he did kill a man once... It was 80 years ago. He saw one of the Egyptian slavedrivers pounding a tired old fellow senseless. And he couldn't stand it! He yelled at the Egyptian to stop, and the fellow just laughed in his face. And Moses' blood boiled, and his adrenalin shot dynamite through his system, and he

127

grabbed hold of that Egyptian and beat him to death! With his bare hands! Sure, Moses had it in him once: the fire of rage. But it didn't explode often. And the older Moses got, the better he kept it under control. In fact, just a couple chapters before this, chapter 12:3, there's a little side-comment about Moses. Miriam and Aaron are trying to pick a fight with him. They're Moses' sister and brother. And they come complaining to him about his wife. Shouldn't have married her, Moses! She's not our kind! And they make fun of her, and they berate him for marrying her! That's enough to get anybody upset.

My Dad knew that. He started farming as a hired hand, after World War II. The man he went to work for died after a short while. And Dad and Mom took over the farm. They rented it from his widow. Her oldest son acted as landlord. For 25 years they worked that land. They watered those acres with their sweat, and they fertilized it with their callouses. And we children learned the meaning of back-breaking toil in those fields. And when, together, we had made that farm produce, the landlord demanded more rent. Now, we had a self-renewing contract, and the rates were already set for that year. But this fellow called and cursed,...he'd come with his pickup truck and park out on the middle of our farmyard, blowing his own horn, till someone would come out to see him. And the worst of it was that he was an Elder in our local church! Doing things like this! To a brother and sister in Christ! But this was the straw that broke the camel's back. Mom never told me. Dad told me later, with pain written all over his face. He refused, at first, to get angry with the man, or to give into all these incredible and unjust demands. But then, when Dad wasn't around, the fellow would come over, and he started calling Mom names! He cursed at her and he berated her cruelly. And that was it. Even though Dad had a legal right to the land, Dad told him to take his farm and shove it! You can argue with me all you want, but when you insult my wife like that...! And Dad was angry!!!

Now get back to Numbers 12. Moses' own brother and sister, Aaron and Miriam, start insulting his wife! And what happens? Does Moses' face go red and puffy? Blisters peal and smoke belch out of his ears? No. We're told that God--God!--got angry with Aaron and Miriam! And that He punished them royally! And that Moses never retaliated! In fact, Moses pleads with God not to be so harsh on them! And the fellow who writes the story in Numbers 12 adds this little comment. Listen! He says: "Now Moses was a very humble man, more humble than anyone else on the face of the earth!" Somewhere along the way Moses had learned to control his temper. And in the process he'd become a very gentle person.

So why was it that Moses hit the stone here?! Who knows? Anger is like a volcano. And deep inside, there's a lake of pain. Pure molten hurt. From the outside no one sees it, usually. We cover it over so well. But one day the heat rises, and the dam breaks, and the cork blows, and anger erupts like an explosion. And rocks get struck. And dogs get kicked. And triggers get pulled. And wives get beaten. And missiles get launched.

Why did Moses hit the rock? Because something in this whole nasty incident rubbed him raw, and the pain demanded an audience.

Five Levels of Pain

What's the pain I'm talking about? Let's see if we can identify it. There are five levels of pain in our lives, actually. And somewhere among them, Moses found the volcano getting out of control.

A. <u>Physical Pain</u> (Sustenance Needs)

129

The first level of pain is physical. Somebody hits me, and I hit him back. It's the rule of the playground, the rule of the hockey ice, the rule of the nursery.

Now, I don't know if Moses was ever knocked about much. But many of us are, at least in our early years. One of the kids on our school bus, when I was young, was Jerome. These days he's a friend of mine. But in those days he was just a mean and tough "big guy." And he had these dark, heavy, black glasses, and he'd take them like this, and he'd grab us little kids by the shoulders, and then he'd drum them on our heads! It hurt an awful lot!

I used to read stories about the Vietnam War. And sometimes, in my darker moments, I'd think about all the booby traps that the Vietcong set up in the jungles. And I'd fantasize about setting some up in our farm grove, and then inviting Jerome to come over some Sunday afternoon... And maybe he'd fall into a pit with poison-tipped bamboo stakes at the bottom... Or maybe he'd step into a snare that would catch his leg and hang him upside-down over a trail of army ants....

You know what I'm talking about! He hurt me, and the pain inside begged to erupt into a mean and vengeful volcano!

B. <u>Emotional Pain</u> (Safety or Security Needs)

The second level of pain is emotional. It's the pain we feel when our security is threatened. Moses knew enough of this pain in his life. For his first few years, he got to stay at home. His mom took care of him, and his sister Miriam looked after him. But the Princess of Egypt had already claimed him, so one day she sent her servants to collect him, and move him to the palace. What happens? What happens to children who bounce around in foster homes? Always a new face...Always a new place...Always a new space...And every child counselor will tell you of the lake of pain that washes around inside.

And then, when Moses killed that Egyptian, and when others found out about it, he ran for his life. He ran, and he ran, and he ran, down to the deserts of Midian. In fact, he ran to someplace around here, where the story takes place in Numbers chapter 20. And maybe it brings back a memory or two. These hills... These caves where he hid... This place that swallowed him up in his painful flight. That was 80 years ago. And what does Moses have to show for his life? He's still a displaced person. He's still on the run from Egypt.

The pain of fear and distrust. It's a big part of Moses' story.

C. Social Pain (Social Needs)

The third level of pain is social. It's the pain that happens when our closest relationships rub raw. If you want a lesson in that watch any of the programs on television that are written and produced by Aaron Spelling. You figure out what they are. Every season he comes out with a whole batch of new ones. And every season at least several become hits. Why? They asked him that in an interview, some time ago, and he said something like this. He said, What I try to do is picture a situation where people have to live together and work together. Maybe they're married, maybe they're friends or office staff, maybe they've just moved in together; but these people will bring out the best in each other, and these people will tear each other to shreds! Aaron Spelling should know! He's got a winning track record on television for 25 years! And he knows the pain of relationships.

Why do husbands beat on wives? Because no anger is more powerful than the anger you direct toward someone you love! Why do family feuds get started, and carry on for years? Because you're bound up in this thing together, and somebody's going to pay for it! How many of you don't find bitterness in your relationship with your parents? Don Posterski and Reginald Bibby interview teenagers across Canada and they asked them about their relationships with their parents: only 2 percent said they could talk with their Dads about something critical in their lives!

And John White, from the University of Manitoba, writes a book that he calls *Parents in Pain*. And Lyman Coleman, who fosters small-group ministries in churches, starts a group that calls itself: "Parenting Adolescents." And Tony Campolo says the most pain he sees as he travels across North America is in the homes of Christians where teens berate parents and where parents humiliate teens.

And the scars of those relationships harden into a cap on the volcano, and keep it from blowing until the next generation. I know a man who hated and despised the way that his father treated him as he was growing up. And now that man treats his own sons exactly the same way. The molten lava of bitterness sloshes around inside. And the emotional pain of family relationships sets it on fire.

Maybe Moses felt that pain grow in him as he walked toward that rock, Aaron his brother at his side. Aaron always tagged along, but he never stood up for anything! Why couldn't he do something, sometime?! Instead he hangs around like a wimp, making idol gods if Moses doesn't always watch him, and grinding at him about his own role as leader! Maybe the emotional pain rages strong this day.

D. Psychological Pain (Self-perspective and Self-worth Needs)

The fourth level of pain is psychological. It's the pain you have inside when someone attacks your self-esteem. Do you think Moses loves his job? I doubt it. You know why? Because he's always been the outsider. When Pharaoh's daughter took him into the palaces of Egypt, Moses lived with his mother's voice whispering in his conscience: Don't forget! You don't belong there! You're not an Egyptian! You're an Israelite! Don't let them suck you in! So for 33 years he lives as an outsider. The other kids of royalty spit on him because he doesn't really have the blood of Pharaoh running in his veins. And the Israelites despise him, because he dresses up all hoity-toity in the fashions of high society, while they drop dead in the stone quarries! And then, when he's 40, the power-brokers of Cairo run him out of town! All his life it's that way. He's too Egyptian to be Israelite. He's too Israelite to be Midianite. He's even too godly to be human. Did you ever think about that? Remember when the people of Israel finally got out of Egypt and they crossed the Red Sea, and they managed to set up camp at Mount Sinai?! God came down on the mountain there, and He wanted to talk to the people. Time for a little chit-chat, a fireside conversation, and God brings His own fire and smoke! And the people get all upset! God's voice is too loud! He shakes the earth too much! The children can't sleep at night! So what do they do?! They come crying to Moses! Moses! they say. Moses! You're better than us! We can't stand to talk to God, but we know that you can! You go, okay?! You go on up the mountain and talk with God for awhile. We'll just sit here doing our ordinary stuff, while you make the Big Guy happy! Suddenly somebody needs Moses! Suddenly the people recognize him as someone special! This is heady stuff! So Moses goes up the mountain. And every step gets brighter! Every time he turns a bend, the heat gets more intense! You can't get this close to God without feeling the power and the glory. And there he is, on top of the mountain, for a whole month and a half! And when he comes down, remember what happens? Here he is, glad to be home again, and the people run away from him! His own children scurry back when he reaches for them and they hide behind Mamma's skirts! Why?! Because his face is glowing like a 1000-watt bulb! Moses is on fire with God's holiness!

Now, think of it! Everybody admires a saint, but nobody loves him! Why? Because he's not like us! Do you know what Paul says in the New Testament? He says that when Moses came down from the mountain they told him to put a bag over his head, so his 1000-watt face wouldn't blind them! Do you see Moses walking around in the camp? He's the guy over there with the big bag on his head! Talk about an identity crisis! And then, says Paul, get this: every morning, when Moses got up, first thing he did was go over to the mirror, and see how the glow was doing. How holy was his face today? How bright was God shining out at the mirror? He'd admire himself and his holiness for awhile and then he'd tuck them back under the bag again, and parade his holiness on the streets of the camp. But then came the morning, a few weeks later, when he looked in the mirror, and the sharpness of the glow was gone. Only about 800 watts staring back at him. And Moses got scared! Would the people respect him anymore? Would they bow to him, and whisper reverently behind his back? So then, says Paul, Moses kept pulling the bag over his head, day after day, week after week, all the while watching the glow disappear: 500 watts; 300 watts; 100 watts; 60, 40, 25... And finally the glow sputtered out altogether, like a nightlight fading in the glow of morning. But what did Moses do? He kept pulling the bag over his head!

Because the people needed a leader who was better than them, someone who stood above them, someone who was more holy than them. And if he ever took the bag off his head, they'd lose their respect for him.

Do you see the pain building in his heart? Always the outsider. Finally getting a little respect. And then losing that too! You see that here. The people come charging up to Moses. They spit in his face! If only we had stayed in Egypt! they say. You did this to us, Moses! It's all your fault!

Years ago, Jim Kok, who's now the Director of Pastoral Care at Garden Grove Community Church in California, (that's the church of "The Hour of Power" television program)...Years ago Jim Kok wrote a little description of the typical background of the typical pastor in the typical church. He said something like this: when he was young, he was kind of quiet and shy, and he didn't get along too well with others of his age. Grownups liked him because he was polite. And in school, even though he was never part of the in-crowd, he found that he could earn the respect of his teachers if he did his homework well. So he grew up as a lonely outsider. And he tried to get people to like him for his holiness and his knowledge. And he spent his life look-ing for a little respect.

There's an awful lot of truth in that. And that's the pain in Moses' heart this day. When will someone just give him a little respect?!

Some time ago the newspapers carried the story of a man driving the highways in one of our major cities. He said that the traffic slowed down as it all funneled into a single lane. And he said that when he got to that point it just inched along. For most of an hour he sat in that lineup. And then, when the road widened again, and the traffic began to move, some jerk bypasses all the stopped cars and comes bouncing along on the shoulder and pulls his car right in front of this man's vehicle! And if that's not enough, the driver of the other car laughs him in the face, and flips him a birdie with his finger! That did it! To be irritated was one thing. But to be taunted and suckered as a fool was quite another. He followed the other car to the next traffic signal. And then he reached into the glove compartment and he pulled out a gun, and he walked up to the other guy's window, and he shot him in the face!

The psychological pain of humiliation caused the volcano of anger to erupt.

E. <u>Meaning Pain</u> (Sanctity Needs)

The highest level of pain is that of our need for meaning in life. On Friday David Irving was deported from Canada. He caused quite a stir here, saying that the Holocaust was a Jewish hoax, that the ovens at Dachau were built after the War as a tourist attraction, that Hitler was a fine fellow. And that kind of talk created a lot of pain in a lot of people.

Simon Wiesenthal writes his little story called *The Sunflower*. He's a young Jewish prisoner. One day the guards separate him from the rest. They lead him through the old city, to a school where he once studied. Now it's a war hospital for German officers. They push him upstairs and around corners. And finally they shove him into a room with a single cot. There's a man lying on that cot, bandaged, but bleeding badly. They leave him alone with the man. He starts talking. His name is Karl. He joined the SS as a volunteer. He loved the life, the excitement, the power. But now he's dying. And before he dies, he's got to get something off his chest. It happened a year ago. They were in a small village, a troop of them. The commander told them to round up the Jews. Bring them to the house at the center of town.

Force them in, twenty, fifty, a hundred and more. Cram them in. Bully them in. Lock them in. They set up a machine gun aimed at the door. Douse the place with gasoline! So they did. Light it! And the flames leaped up. And there they stood in a ring around the house, all those SS soldiers. And they pulled their pistols. And the Jews in the house screamed. And some of them tried to jump out of the second-floor windows. And a man held a child in his arms. And his clothes were on fire. And he wrapped his hand over the boy's head. And he jumped to the ground below, rolling to protect the lad. And we fired our guns. Oh God! the dying man said, I shot that boy! And all the while Simon Wiesenthal is getting more and more upset. Why is he telling me this?! What does he want from me?! And then it comes out. The man sobs. He cries. His chest throbs with torment. He knows he's dying. But he's scared. He's scared to die with this horror staining his hands. Forgive me! he says. You've got to forgive me! You're a Jew, and you've got to forgive me for those people, for that child!....

What would you do? Do you know? Here's Simon Wiesenthal. And he wasn't in that house. And he wasn't ever hurt by this man. At least not physically or emotionally. But can he do this thing? The man attacks the very core of his being! Can he forgive this man and still find any meaning to his life?

This is pain at its deepest. This is Moses' pain with God. Why? Why, why, why? Is there some purpose to all this madness?

And the heart of Moses erupts with painful anger. And Moses slaps his staff against the rock.

Three Kinds of Anger
Do you find yourself somewhere in this story? Do you know the bloating of a lake of pain in your heart, a

lake of pain that seethes on the verge of eruption every now and again? I know when I seethe. I think you probably know it too.

One psychotherapist says that anger is the most pervasive difficulty troubling his patients. Ours is an angry society, he says, and it comes out in three ways.

A. Revenge

Sometimes it's Revenge. You know, the bumper stickers that say: I don't get mad; I get even! When they were digging in the earth, some years ago, expanding the runways at Boston's airport, they uncovered the basement remains of an old house. A 19th century house. A house that held a horror. A house with an extra room in the basement, walled over and hidden. And in that room, a skeleton. The remains of a man clawing at the bricks, trying to find a way out. And when they checked the records of the house, they found that at one time this house had been occupied by none other than Edgar Allen Poe. Think of that next time you read his little tale called "The Cask of Amontillado." The story of a rich man named Montresor who invited his seeming friend Fortunato to an evening of eating and drinking. And left him alone and drunk in a basement room. And walled up the doorway in front of him. And left him there to die. Because Montresor thought that Fortunato had insulted and belittled him.

Who do you think Moses was beating when he struck the rock?! It had nothing to do with that big chunk of granite. Moses was striking out at the people of Israel. Because they had pushed him once too much. And the pain swelled inside. And the volcano erupted. And Moses' anger spilled out all over the place in revenge.

B. Rage

Sometimes it's rage. Remember when James Huberty went into that McDonald's restaurant in San

Diego? Usually a nice family place to go. But not that morning. He was always angry, said his wife. There was a rage inside of him, said his neighbors. His mother left him in childhood--emotional pain! His only friend had died the year before--social pain! He lost his job earlier that week--psychological pain! And the volcano erupted. And the hot rock exploded. And more than twenty men, women, and children died in its killing flames.

This is the pain that simmers in the soul of the wife-beater. Not long ago someone in our own community broke his wife's nose, twisted her arm out of joint, and threw an axe at her through the windshield of their vehicle. He's in jail now. But his rage simmers just under the surface. It pools in the lake of pain that he's gathered to himself over the years. And unless something drains that lake, he'll break out in rage again down the road.

Recently someone collected strange insurance claims and turned them into a book. Here's the police report from an accident site: "Suspect drove her vehicle into: eighteen parked cars, four moving vehicles, two stop signs, one trailer truck, all between Sycamore and Rose Avenues. Suspect said she was mad at her boyfriend." (*Incredible Insurance Claims*) Maybe she felt a little like Moses that day!

C. <u>Resentment</u>

But the granddaddy of them all, in terms of all of us here, is probably the third volcanic rupture. It's only a little fissure in the side of the mountain, seething in slow-moving streams, an acrid smelling flow of resentment.

Maybe you saw it last week in *The Banner*. Dr. Harry Van Belle wrote about the struggles of church life in the Christian Reformed denomination right now. He said there's probably a reason for the church splits that are happening. He said there's always a lot of pain in immigration. And those who make the move have most to lose. They lost their place in the old country. They rarely do find a place in the new country. And along the way they often lose their youth. Too much work to do. Too many lessons to learn. Too great a price to pay. And they pay the price. And they settle for being aliens in a strange world. Except in the church. They can hang onto that. They can make it a bulwark of stability in the middle of this vast, teeming, troubled ocean of change. And for a while it works. Life swirls around this one calm center of safety and familiarity. And then it happens. The church begins to change too. And the panic sets in. And the resentment grows. And sometimes the volcano erupts.

There's something unholy and ungodly about a resentful life. Not that a person with a dour outlook can't do much good, or be much loved by God. But resentment shows unresolved pain. And that pain of heart keeps any one of us from fully experiencing the grace of God. Why do you think God promises us a life beyond this one? Because Moses needs another start, with another heart. Because I need another start, with another heart. Because you need another start, with another heart. And the trouble with some of our lives here is that we've loved too little, worshipped too little, sang too little, laughed too little, enjoyed too little, because the lake of pain inside came out constantly in the darker streams of resentment and woe and bitterness.

Discharging the Volcano

According to recent medical research, angry people, whether they show it in revenge or rage or resentment, have a 20 percent shorter lifespan than those who can come to terms with the lake of pain inside. The pain eats away, and just as Moses showed, it'll come out somewhere, sometime, in ways that hurt.

What do you do with the pain under the volcano? Revenge can't really heal it. Recently a man who had raped, robbed, and murdered a 16-year-old girl was put to death in the U.S. The girl's father demanded to be there when they fried him in the electric chair. And after the ordeal, a reporter interviewed him. This is what he said. He said: Dying isn't enough..for him! He said: I wanted him to suffer more for what he did to my daughter! Revenge never soothes the pain. It only bloodies the battlefield. But suppressing the pain won't do it either. Psychologists tell us that the major reason for depression in our society is suppressed anger. It soils the soul. It harries the heart. It sulks in the spirit. Nor will "acting out" the rage defuse it, as some think. If you punch a bag with the face of your boss on it, if you give your golf balls the names of your enemies, if you vent your resentment at your spouse, chances are you'll only feed your rage.

So what can you do? Two things, probably.

For one thing, we've got to identify the pain that broods inside. Sometimes, when I come home after a particularly troubling day, I storm at Brenda, and I'm short and mean with our daughters. It happens. And the best thing that Brenda can do is to ask: So how was your day? And I'll rage a bit. But usually I'll tell her a bit, also, what happened that fed the fires inside. And knowing what I'm angry about helps to keep me from being angry in the wrong ways.

141

One preacher tells of a couple he came to know a bit. And it seemed as if the woman was always scolding her husband. She could call him all sorts of names. Even in public, she'd often berate him. The preacher was amazed at the way the man took it all. One day he asked the husband about it, why he put up with that kind of painful treatment. And this is what the man said. He said that a few years before their son died tragically. Cancer. Painful. Wasted away. And ever since, he said, his wife had been angry with God for letting it happen. He said that she couldn't seem to fight it out with God. So now she took it out on him. And in the quietness of that confession showed the strength of great compassion. The pain will come out. The volcano will erupt. And blessed are those who know why.

The second thing we have to do is this: learn to reframe. Learn to take the picture that reminds us of our pain, and then put it in a new frame. A frame of God's eternal justice. A frame of Christ's incredible forgiveness. A frame of the Spirit's redeeming mercy and grace and love.

It's more than just counting to ten when you're angry. Thomas Jefferson said: When angry, count to ten; when very angry, count to one hundred. Mark Twain had another version. He said: When angry, count to four; when very angry, swear! And then there's the claim on an insurance form. It says: "Whenever I get angry, I close my eyes and count to 10. I was mad at my brother while I was driving... And I closed my eyes, and the next thing I knew, there was this terrible crash!" (Brian Herbert, *Incredible Insurance Claims*, Price/Stearn/Sloan Publishers, 1982)

Reframing is more than that. It's taking the fire out of the lake of pain inside by injecting the transforming grace of forgiveness and love. Some years ago a

26-year-old Korean graduate student at the University of Pennsylvania stepped out of his apartment to mail a letter home. On his way back, a gang of teens robbed him and killed him. In Korea, the young man's mother was deeply hurt. Her congregation raised the money to send her to America. While in Philadelphia, she went to the trial of those who had killed her son. They laughed at her and insulted her with cruel jokes. The legal system handed down a murder verdict for all of them. And then the strange thing happened: when the judge laid sentence and called for the death penalty, the mother actually fell on her knees in front of him. She pleaded with him to spare their lives. And at her tears for them, the murderers found themselves weeping. And the judge. And the whole courtroom. Because they didn't know what to do with anger that had been transformed into grace, and into forgiveness, and into love.

I don't know what lake of pain burns in your soul. I know there's a pool there in my life. Sometimes it grows. Sometimes it shrinks. Sometimes I find myself relishing revenge on someone who hurts me. Sometimes I find my cork popping in rage that's often vented at my family. And sometimes I seethe in resentment over what I've had to suffer.

I know what it's like to stand with Moses on that rock. I know what he feels. And I know why God shook His head that day and called him on it. Because anger is the volcanic eruption of pain, and pain is the lake of fire swimming around inside each of us. And somewhere along the way, we'll only be able to find more to our lives when we've truly seen that pain, and when we've been able to reframe it in the message of the gospel of grace.